The Little Red Yellow Black Book

An introduction to Indigenous Australia

Aboriginal
Studies
Press

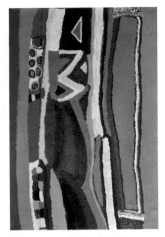

Birrmuyingathi Maali Netta
Loogatha, *My Sister Amy's
Country.*

Aboriginal and Torres Strait Islander peoples
are respectfully advised that this publication
contains the names and images of deceased
people. The Australian Institute of Aboriginal
and Torres Strait Islander Studies (AIATSIS)
apologises for any distress this may inadvertently
cause.

AIATSIS is the world's premier institution for
information and research about the cultures
and lifestyles of Aboriginal and Torres Strait
Islander peoples.

The Institute undertakes and encourages
scholarly, ethical community-based research,
holds a priceless collection of films, photographs, video and audio recordings and the
world's largest collections of printed and other
resource materials for Indigenous Studies, as
well as having its own publishing house.

Its activities affirm and raise awareness
among all Australians, and people of other
nations, of the richness and diversity of
Australian Indigenous cultures and histories.

Contents

Welcome

It is a mark of respect for Aboriginal and Torres Strait Island people to welcome visitors to their land.

Today, some civic ceremonies across the country begin with a welcoming of people to country by a traditional owner. Indigenous Australians acknowledge when they're on the land of traditional owners and some non-Indigenous Australians do the same. These gestures of respect acknowledge Indigenous ownership and custodianship of the land, their traditions and their ancestors.

In accordance with this courtesy, we welcome you to this book and acknowledge all of the traditional owners whose country we talk about.

Noongar man, Shane Abdullah, performing at the welcome ceremony, AIATSIS Native Title Conference (Koorah, Yira, Boordah; Past, Present, Future) 2008.

How to Use this Book

We have written *The Little Red Yellow Black Book* so that all Australians (and visitors) might learn of our connection to this land in the hope that we might prosper together as a nation in full knowledge and acceptance of our shared history. It is a revised and expanded edition of a book published in 1994.

The book offers an introduction to our culture and, as such, it can offer only a mere snapshot of our histories, cultures and identities. Our website, http://lryb.aiatsis.gov.au, provides information we did not have space to include here, including photos and audiovisual material, teachers' notes and ideas for further reading.

As Aboriginal and Torres Strait Islander people we continue to maintain our strong and different identities, so it is impossible to produce a single narrative, or to include everyone's story. As with all communities, not all of us agree about the past, and some of us disagree with what non-Indigenous commentators have said about us. Our aim is to provide information about our history and culture in an approachable way. The underlying themes that emerge are our adaptability and the vitality and continuity of our cultures. We think you will find much to surprise, interest and inform you, and we hope you will enjoy reading it.

Some of us live in remote communities but many more of us live in regional towns and cities. We hope that Aboriginal and Torres Strait Islander readers will recognise their histories, their communities and their lives in this book, and that non-Indigenous people, whether Australian or from overseas, gain some insights into what may well be the world's most enduring cultural practices.

We use words such as 'coloniser', rather than 'settler', because it was the intention of the British Government to take control and ownership of this continent, which had been our home since time immemorial. After the initial waves of colonisation (some of us call it an invasion) and much subsequent frontier violence, the British 'settled' the country. Over the decades since then, new waves of people have arrived on our shores and become Australians.

When we talk about 'war', we don't mean trench warfare or large-scale clashes between tens of thousands of soldiers; rather, we mean guerilla tactics, where two forces of unequal power oppose each other, but not with armies on a battlefield.

This may be language you are not used to hearing when we talk about history. But it is important that we present our experience of this shared history.

We have cross-referenced parts of the book to other sections to show the links across themes. References are included for further reading. We hope you're encouraged to undertake your own research after reading the book, the better to participate in, and accept, our shared history and humanity.

Who Are We?

Our Past

When asked where we come from, our usual response is: we have always been here. Successive archaeological discoveries reveal the truth of this statement. Researchers now say that our ancestors lived on the Torres Strait islands for more than 10000 years and on the mainland for over 60000 years — a longer period than modern humans have been in many parts of Europe and the Americas.

From what is known today, it's clear that Aboriginal Australians have adapted over time to a range of climatic and environmental changes, including those brought about by their extensive use of fire. While culture could never have been static, a level of stability and continuity became the norm thousands of years prior to Europeans arriving. With few exceptions, though, such regional differences in social and cultural forms can be easily recognised as variants of a number of basic themes shared right across the continent, and unique to Australia. No other continent on earth has this level of homogeneity, and we are unique among the world's hunter–gatherers for the sheer complexity of our social organisation and religion.

Cave art and stone petroglyphs (carvings or inscriptions in rock) in Australia may be the first representations of this type of art anywhere in the world. Some forms of ground-stone axe manufacture probably began in the Australian continent earlier than elsewhere and, along with its other technologies, saw adaptive and sophisticated developments.

It will be fascinating for young black and white Australian researchers to further examine this history, an ancient heritage that should be a source of pride for all Australians.

The Bardi Dancers from Ardiyooloon community (formerly One Arm Point) perform the Corroborree Billy Ah choo Ilma at Stonehenge. Five generations took part in the Salisbury International Arts Festival 2006. L–R: Moochoo Davey, Lyle Davey, Brent Mouda and Cojie Ahchoo.

It is estimated that there are between 500,000 and one million Aboriginal petroglyphs (rock engravings) on the Burrup Peninsula, Western Australia.

What We're Called

Because our ancestors always identified themselves in local or regional terms, there was never a single name for all of us until we were labelled 'Aborigines' by the British. *Aborigine* is from a Latin phrase meaning *in a place*, while *Indigenous* means *originating in and characterising a particular region.*

An Aboriginal person is often defined legally as a person who is a descendant of an Indigenous inhabitant of Australia, sees himself or herself as an Aboriginal person and is recognised as Aboriginal by members of the community in which he or she lives. Many visitors to this country are not aware that we have two Indigenous peoples. Torres Strait Islanders, whose cultural origins are in nearby Melanesia, lived traditionally in the Torres Strait, which separates the north of Queensland from New Guinea. Of the more than 100 islands in the Strait, nineteen are inhabited by a total of twenty communities, which include the Northern Peninsula Area (Cape York). Many Torres Strait Islanders have migrated and today live throughout mainland Australia.

WHAT WE CALL OURSELVES

Government officials and other people who want a word to include both Aboriginal and Torres Strait Islander peoples use 'Indigenous Australians' or 'Indigenous peoples'. This language is also used in the United Nations, who refer to Indigenous peoples from all around the world. When referring to ourselves, we use a variety of broad, regional 'tribal' or linguistic labels. For example, those of us from New South Wales and Victoria might call ourselves Kooris, Queenslanders Murris, or, in the north, Bama, Tasmanians Palawa, South Australians Nunga and south-west Australians use Nyoongars (also Nyungar). (There can be different spellings to some of these words.) Those of us living on the coast call ourselves 'saltwater' and others 'freshwater' people. But many of us would rather be identified by a language label; for example, a Gurindji man or a Gubbi Gubbi woman. Torres Strait Islanders prefer to use the name of their islands to identify themselves to outsiders; for example, a Badulayg or a Meriam. Socio-political groupings are also common in the native title era — by definition these groups are bound by their laws and customs. This can be reflected in the use of the word 'nations' or 'peoples'.

When referring to Australia's Indigenous people it is acceptable to say 'Aboriginal people', 'Torres Strait Islanders' or 'Indigenous people'. When written, these labels are capitalised. You may sometimes hear us referring to ourselves as 'blackfellas' in a joking, non-derogatory way. However, we advise you not to use it unless you know your audience well.

Living with our Neighbours

In 1606 both Dutch and Spanish vessels were voyaging within sight of the Australian coast. Sailing from Callao in Peru in 1605, Luis de Torres was second in command of the *San Pedrico*, which navigated its way through the sometimes dangerous reefs and islands of the Torres Strait. He sighted the hills of Cape York but took them to be a cluster of islands. The Dutch vessel *Duyfken*, commanded by Willem Jansz, was in the Torres Strait weeks before de Torres but proceeded no further than Cape Keer-weer (Cape Turn-again), on the north-west side of the Cape York Peninsula. The Dutchman Willem van Colster's exploratory voyage in 1623 is the first recorded contact with Europeans in Arnhem Land.

Despite cultural and linguistic differences, the Yolngu people of East Arnhem Land traded with Macassan sailors for hundreds of years before European ships ventured to our shores. Using the monsoon winds, the Macassans sailed from Sulawesi, one of the largest islands in East Indonesia, seeking trepang (sea cucumber). In exchange, they offered the Yolngu metal knives, cloth and tobacco.

The Macassans were seasonal visitors, who came to trade but did not invade, and the clashes that occurred seem to have been an exception to a relationship that worked well, socially and economically, for both peoples. These visits are still recorded and celebrated in the music and dance of the Yolngu and other northern language groups.

Some of us joined the visitors when they went back to their own country, and marriages with the Macassans cemented the connection. We adopted the use of some words like *balanda* for white or lighter-skinned people (from the Macassan word for *Hollander*) and some items like bamboo, clay pipes and glass. Further east, in the Torres Strait, the Islanders enjoyed one of the richest marine environments in the world, with fish, crustaceans, turtles, and in some parts, dugong ('sea cows'). Land resources were more variable, so inter-island trading networks enabled Islanders to obtain what they lacked and to redistribute surpluses. They also exchanged valued items, like cassowary feathers, drums and ochres.

The Islanders' ocean-going canoes, often in small fleets, allowed them to travel far afield. In return for pearl shell, cone shell, turtle shell and stone they obtained canoe hulls, up to 20 metres long, from Papua. To these they added double outriggers and their own distinctive form of rigging which allowed them to become maritime explorers engaged in long-distance trading. They navigated by the stars and used their intimate knowledge of the islands and their reefs, the weather, tides and currents. Also from Papua came drums, though the Islanders made their own special curved shark-mouth drums. The Southern islanders traded with the Aboriginal people of Cape York to obtain spears, spear throwers and ochre, while food and decorative ornaments were traded between the islands. Songs, dances and esoteric objects and knowledge (such as magical spells) were also carried and exchanged along these trade routes.

After the foundation of the British colony in New South Wales, the Torres Strait became a common route for ships, if a dangerous one, because of the reefs and raiding parties led by our warriors. Sailors commented on the Islanders' warlike attitude.

'Macassan' painting by Charlie Matjuwi features a Macassan boat, trepang, and swords traded to Yolngu people. Macassan interaction with Yolngu communities is still remembered through story, song and art.

By the 1800s, some of the foreign visitors, most of whom were seeking to exploit the sea's resources, including seamen from the Philippines, married Torres Strait Island women, but most intermarriages were with other Pacific Islanders, including Rotumans, Samoans, New Hebrideans (Vanuatu) and Lifuans (Noumea).

Our Societies

Our world view

The Dreaming is a unique religious concept, but it goes well beyond the ordinary sense we understand dreams to be. Altered states of consciousness, like dreams, play a vital part in the transmission of knowledge between the spiritual and human realms. For Aboriginal people, the Dreaming refers to the creation period (a time beyond human memory) when ancestral beings are said to have spread across the continent, creating human society and its rules for living, language and customs and laws as they went. Great magicians, huge and beautiful (many having both human and animal qualities simultaneously), turned a flat, featureless plain into the wonderful and varied topography we admire today. Tired by all their endeavours, they eventually 'died' as bodies, but their spiritual essence remains, in the landscape, the heavens, and the waters. We believe that their life-giving and life-sustaining powers exist at important places to this day. Our culture is based on a kind of contract: that we must follow the ancestral dictates (we use the English word 'Law' to mean this entire cultural inheritance, its injunctions and taboos and rules for life) in order to stimulate and guarantee the continued flow of fertility and power from the spiritual realm. Our great founding ancestral beings are still 'out there', not interfering directly, but ever watchful. We gain our personal spirit, the life-force that animates us, ultimately from the actions of these beings. Through the performance of our ceremonies we are calling on the creative powers to keep the land fertile, to maintain the seasons and ensure the well-being of us all. Although the Dreaming refers to creation events of the past, it is the 'everywhen', embracing the past, present

Mac Gardiner and his great-great-grandson Charles Croydon return earth to Martu country in Western Australia.

and future. On ritual occasions, art and song celebrate this central connection between the creator beings, ancestral country and us. The Dreaming is an enduring life-force, even though individuals come and go, and lives change. Many of us retain this essential religious outlook. Both as individuals and as members of social groups, we have a great many different connections to particular 'Dreamings', such as plants, animals and other elements of nature.

Torres Strait Islanders believed in and are connected to one another by *Cult Heroes*, ancestral beings who criss-crossed the Torres Strait. Through them, Torres Strait Islanders are linked to each other and to the peoples of southern New Guinea and northern Queensland. The Cult Heroes gave Torres Strait Islanders laws to live by and laws that taught respect for each other, the earth and the sea. Some of the ancestors were said to be shape-shifters — at times human, at other times animal, reptile, bird or fish. This ability allowed the ancestor to dwell in, and travel through, water, earth, oil, sea and air. Like these beings, Torres Strait Islanders understand themselves to be intimately connected to the land and sea environments that are their home. These connections are everyday ones that are reinforced through fishing, gardening and turtle and dugong hunting.

Some Heroes turned into places in the sea, land or sky. Today, for example, Torres Strait Islanders look up to the warrior Tagai in the night

THE DREAMING

Mussolini Harvey, a Yanyuwa man from the Gulf of Carpentaria, tells it this way:

In our language, Yanyuwa, we call the Dreaming Yijan. The Dreamings made our Law or narnu-Yuwa. This Law is the way we live, our rules. This Law is our ceremonies, our songs, our stories; all of these things came from the Dreaming. One thing that I can tell you though is that our Law is not like European law which is always changing — new government, new laws; but our Law cannot change, we did not make it. The Law was made by the Dreamings many, many years ago and given to our ancestors and they gave it to us.

The Dreamings are our ancestors, no matter if they are fish, birds, men, women, animals, wind or rain. It was these Dreamings that made our Law. All things in our country have Law, they have ceremony and song, and they have people who are related to them.

The Dreamings named all of the country and the sea as they travelled, they named everything that they saw. As the Dreamings travelled they put spirit children over the country, we call these spirit children *ardirri*. It is because of these spirit children that we are born, the spirit children are on the country, and we are born from the country. In our ceremonies we wear marks on our bodies, they come from the Dreaming too, we carry the design that the Dreamings gave to us.

Nganyintja Ilyatjari, a Pitjantjatjara woman from the country around Mount Davies, describes it this way:

Our country, the country out there near Mount Davies, is full of sacred places. The Kangaroo Dreaming has been there since the beginning, the Wild Fig Dreaming has been there since the beginning, many other women's Dreamings are also there. In other places men and women's Dreamings were together from a long time ago.

skies. Depending on his position, they know when the seasonal rains will come and when they should plant crops. When Tagai's left hand (the Southern Cross) moves towards the sea the season's first rain, *kuki*, begins.

Our connections to our land

Our traditional mode of social and economic organisation is known as 'hunting and gathering', by far humanity's most enduring adaptation. This way of life depends fundamentally on mobility so as not to exhaust resources at any one place, and to take advantage of a range of ecotypes. Despite its size, the continent lacked plants and animals that could be domesticated. Our rights to land were recognised by the High Court's *Mabo* decision in 1992, which said that, according to Australian law, Indigenous people have rights to land, rights that existed before colonisation and endure (see p. 116).

THE STORY OF TAGAI

One day Tagai and his crew of Zugubals (beings who took on human form when they visited Earth) were fishing from their outrigger canoe. They caught no fish, and so Taga , being the best fisherman, went to a nearby reef to fish there.

The Zugubals grew hot as they waited. They dived into the water but were still hot so they dragged Tagai's coconut shells full of water into the canoe and drank from them.

Tagai was angry that they had drunk all the water for the voyage, so he killed all twelve crew members. He placed them in two groups in the night sky — Usal (the Pleiades) and Utimal (Orion) — and told them to stay in the northern sky, away from him.

Nowadays, if the crew wish to appear in the eastern sky, they cause thunder and lightning as a signal. Hearing this, Tagai dips below the western horizon.

Aboriginal culture seems paradoxical to scholars who specialise in the study of human societies. Traditionally, we were both mobile and very strongly connected culturally, in multiple and complex ways, to particular sites and country that comprised our 'tribal' homeland. We have obligations and responsibilities for particular areas of land. We often use the English word 'country', and it is a fundamental element of our culture and identity.

All of us are connected to the land through our Dreamings. Although the forces of colonisation destroyed much of that connection as the settler frontier spread through the continent, many communities are working hard to re-establish the links that underpinned identity and provided a sense of security and pride in belonging to, and caring for, country.

Family ties

Some Aboriginal people, particularly those in rural and remote regions of the continent, have managed to retain very complex familial systems. Other groups, in areas that were colonised earliest and most intensively, are no longer enmeshed in large, dense networks of kin. Dislocation, institutionalisation, removal from parents and other factors have played a part. The establishment of Link-Up organisations, which now operate in every state means that expert assistance is now available to those of us trying to locate missing relatives. For many, finding out about family can be both challenging and rewarding. Today, at the Australian Institute of Aboriginal and Torres Strait Islander Studies (AIATSIS), in Canberra, there is a Family History Unit, which helps people to trace their Indigenous family history.

Many Aboriginal people do family history work. Ngarrindjeri elder and researcher, Doreen Kartinyeri, made good use of the genealogies and information provided by anthropologist Norman Tindale (1900–93) about her people in South Australia. Alick Jackomos (1924–99) was a non-Aboriginal man with an Aboriginal family, whose work is drawn on by Victorian Aboriginal families today. He travelled widely, taking and collecting photos, hundreds of which are in the AIATSIS archives, along with more than a thousand intricate family trees that he recorded.

Aboriginal traditional owner and elder of Nyikina country, John Watson shows his grandchildren his special lands in Western Australia's Kimberley area.

FAMILY AND ELDERS

We honour and respect the role of our elders, who look after the land in accordance with the directions of our ancestors. Drug and alcohol abuse have undermined the authority of elders in many communities, but we know from experience that when a community returns to good health, good education and lasting jobs, the voice of our elders is also reinstated. Their traditional role continues into the modern world, where they are crucial to all decision making in the community, from protecting our culture and extended families down to choosing who drives the school bus or represents the community at a government inquiry. Our respect for elders is shown in common forms of address, where 'Uncle' or 'Aunty', reflect respect and deference to the generations that preceded us.

In some areas, where these systems are still in use, Aboriginal people belong to *skin-groups*. People are born into these categories, and they are useful mainly when grouping people for rituals, as naming labels, and as guides to a person's likely relationship to others. Some Aboriginal groups in central and northern Australia still use skin-group categories as guides to appropriate behaviour towards others, and they indicate intermarrying categories. Some of us are linked as part of a descent group, where each group relates to an area where a particular creative being lived or travelled. We inherit rights in land and Dreamings in a variety of ways, including through our mother, father, grandparents, place of conception or birth, or adoption.

Island communities

In the Torres Strait, each community was traditionally divided into a number of descent (or clan) groups that traced descent through the father's line (similar to southern Papua) and wives were drawn from groups other than one's own. Each group had a name and was associated with a place and, with the Central and Western Islanders, with an ancestral totem. Men, in particular, maintained a quest for spiritual power and

Fishing charms from Saibi Island Torres Strait, 1898.

THE MYTH OF WIDUL AND MARTE AND THEIR BROTHER UMAI

Once upon a time, two sisters, Widul and Marte, lived with their brother Umai at the north-west end of Mabuiag Island. Widul had a daughter named Sarabar, and Marte had a daughter named Iadi.

One day Widul and Marte quarrelled. Widul threw a spear at Marte, which split her down the middle, at the same instant as Marte threw several spears at Widul. Marte's spears split the top of Widul's skull and struck into it.

Umai put a stop to the fight between the two sisters — as their brother, he had the right, and duty to do it — by moving them far apart from each other and sending them to places of his choosing on the reef which surrounds Mabuiag.

The sisters and their daughters became islands. Umai turned to stone and has ever since stood guard over them at the edge of the passage through the reef between Marte and another island, Aipus. He can be seen at low tide. Widul stays south of Umai and keeps her small daughter, Sarabar, behind her. Marte's place is north of him, and she also keeps her daughter, Iadi, behind her.

For a long time, pandanus trees grew at the top of Marte — they were the spears that were thrown at her by her sister, Widul.

made use of magic to aid gardening, hunting and sailing. Rivalry was fierce between some Islanders, some of it more a matter of fighting for show than actual fighting, but fear of sorcery was real. Despite this, the Islanders often came together to trade, for rituals (including dancing), to enhance social relationships and for enjoyment. Life was to change with the Coming of the Light, when Christian missionaries arrived in 1871 and put an end to some of the old ways of life, the warfare and the old cults. Today, Christianity remains strong in Torres Strait Islander communities, and a major ceremonial is the Coming of the Light. Recreating the arrival of the first missionaries on Erub (Darnley Island), each year this ritual is performed by Islanders who come together to celebrate, whether in the Islands or on the mainland.

Living off the land and sea

The British colonised mainland Australia as if it were *terra nullius* (land belonging to no one) but this ignored our systems of land ownership, and intimate attachment to, the entire continent. Today, you can still see some of the old stone tunnels, channels and ponds we used to modify waterways in Arnhem Land and the Kimberley, and stone fish traps around Mer, Erub and Ugar islands in the Torres Strait. The Gunditjmara people of western Victoria conduct tours of the water-races (canals) made by their forebears and the stone dwellings they lived in during the fishing season.

In Australia, Aboriginal people traditionally lived in small mobile groups or 'bands', and our ranges of movement and population densities had much to do with the nature and distribution of natural resources. Groups tended to be small and widely scattered in desert areas, while communities on well-watered coasts and in the lower River Murray region were relatively sedentary. On the eastern Cape York Peninsula, in the dry season people moved inland in small groups to hunt, gather and fish.

We used the resources of the land and sea. Some of us travelled widely, using our extensive knowledge of the seasons and weather to work out when the best time was to move to a different location. All groups knew the movements of others and larger groups gathered for ceremonies or to feast on particular foods that would be plentiful at certain times of year.

We are experts in the use of fire to manage our country, using low-intensity fires to clear the undergrowth, promote the regrowth of some plants and encouraging grazing and easier spearing by game animals. Much of the land has long been modified by this regular burning in favour of species that recover quickly. Certain yam and seed-producing plants benefit from burning. Kangaroos, particularly, like to eat the new growth of grass. *Firestick farming*, as it is now called, is a purposeful

Kuninjku people hunting on their country at Marrkolidjban
near Maningrida in Arnhem Land, Northern Territory
© Luke Taylor.

strategy for intensifying the availability of edible food, and is an essential feature of caring for country.

Aboriginal people were frequently on the move, so their toolkits were lightweight and multipurpose. Hunters used carved wooden hunting tools like spears, clubs and boomerangs. Women carried digging sticks and wooden containers or baskets. In some areas their spinning and weaving produced twine, nets and bags for carrying food. Nowadays in remote communities some women prefer using iron digging sticks and men favour guns which make it easier to hunt large animals like buffalo, cattle, camels and pigs that have run wild on Aboriginal lands.

We still catch or gather many of the traditional foods today: turtle, dugong, shellfish, magpie geese, grain, fruits, tubers, file snakes, oysters, mussels, duck, kangaroo, echidna, murnong (yam daisy), eels, salmon, whiting, abalone, mullet and shark. Some foods, like dugong and turtle, are found only in the north while others, like abalone and eels, are more common in the south of the country.

The Scottish-born explorer John McKinlay (1819–72) saw people herd baby pelicans into a brush yard, keep them and use the young birds for food just before they could fly. Other explorers record seeing us pulping figs into a long-lasting preserved cake. Meat was dried, smoked and salted. We dug yams and promoted the growth of other tubers where we found them. We have vast stores of knowledge about

AN EXPLORER'S DIARY

While searching for the missing explorer Ludwig Leichhardt and exploring further afield in 1855–56, Augustus Charles Gregory wrote that:

field[s] of 1,000 acres [400 hectares] are there met with growing this cereal. The natives cut it down by means of stone knives, cutting down the stalk half way, beat out the seed, leaving the straw, which is often met in large heaps.

Around the start of the twentieth century, Walter Smith, a carrier, dogger and miner in the Western Desert country, witnessed how watercourses were diverted:

the people would get in a line, using their digging-scoops and larger coolamons. The clay and earth was scooped into larger coolamons, which were passed along the line (in a speedy operation) . . . While some deepened the catchment area, others built a bank, simultaneously. People would trample the clay base. If ant nest material was nearby this was carried in to give a very firm base.'

how to live on this continent, and part of this is revealed in the diaries of the non-Indigenous explorers, which in some cases offer detailed descriptions of hunting and gathering activities, like firestick farming.

Sharing food

Aboriginal people used to visit and care for specific localities to take advantage of seasonal foods and many communities continue this practice today. When these foods — cycad palms in the north, bogong moths in the Alps, grain harvests of the inland, eel trapping in the south, crayfish and shellfish collections on the coast — were at their most plentiful, it was an occasion to invite neighbours to share the bounty. These gatherings were announced by messengers who were given the right to travel safely through the lands of others. These gatherings allowed us to trade, acquire and exchange new songs, dances, valued

BUSH TUCKER

Bush tucker is the food Aboriginal people lived on prior to colonisation. It includes edible plants, nuts, tubers, fruits, seafood and game. While looking for plants containing vitamin B, James Cook found the plant Bower Spinach (sometimes called Cook's spinach, Warrigal cabbage or New Zealand spinach) growing on the roofs of Aboriginal dwellings. Some people living semi-traditional lives still harvest honey, tubers, seeds and pandanus nuts. Visitors who take our culture tours will be shown many of these foods.

artefacts and other forms of culture, to meet relatives and to arrange marriages.

All members of our communities had particular responsibilities for collecting and preparing food, and the division of labour was largely gender-based: men usually hunted large game while women hunted small game and gathered food. Depending on the area and the season, we had access to highly nutritious food.

The Torres Strait islands vary in their geography and their capacity to sustain people, some having little water and poor soil. The trade of food and other items was strong between islands, and with people further afield (see p. 90).

The Eastern Islanders were able to grow yams, bananas and other crops. In the Western Island there were wild yams and other edible roots, as well as mangrove pods. The Central Islanders were less well off but they traded with other islands. Throughout the islands, our protein came from the sea: in particular, molluscs, fish, turtle and dugong.

Changes to traditional lifestyles

For Aboriginal people, the fencing of land by the colonists restricted our access to fresh water. When the colonists let their animals out to graze on the land or drained swamps to make more pasture, many staple vegetable foods disappeared, reducing variety in our diet and increasing the risk of deficiencies and disease.

For instance, sheep cropped the basal leaves of the yam daisy (murrnong) so closely that it disappeared completely from most districts of south-eastern Australia. We lost access to some of the basic components of our diet, and came to prefer the colonisers' less nutritious white flour, tea and sugar. The impact of the disappearance or restricted access to food cannot be underestimated (see p. 91).

By the 1820s and 1830s, some Torres Strait Island communities were in contact with passing European ships. They traded fresh food and other items for iron. Trepangers, those seeking bêche-de-mer or sea cucumber (considered an aphrodisiac by Chinese people), were working in the Torres Strait from the 1860s for long periods, sometimes in great numbers. They were equipped with guns, and the Islanders were at a disadvantage against these better-armed invaders. Between the London Missionary Society and the government, the Torres Strait was transformed during the last quarter of the nineteenth century; however, except for the Kauarareg, most Torres Strait Islanders were able to stay on their island lands.

Languages

More than 200 distinct languages, and countless dialects of them, were in use when European settlement began. The ancestral creative beings were said to have left languages on the country, along with the first humans and their culture. It was usual for people to speak at least one or more neighbouring languages besides their own. In some areas, like Arnhem Land, many different languages were spoken over a small area, whereas at the other extreme, in the huge Western Desert, which covers about one sixth of the continent, dialects of only one language are spoken.

Sadly, only a small number of our languages are spoken fluently today. While people in some communities continue to speak their own languages, many others are seeking to record and revive threatened ones.

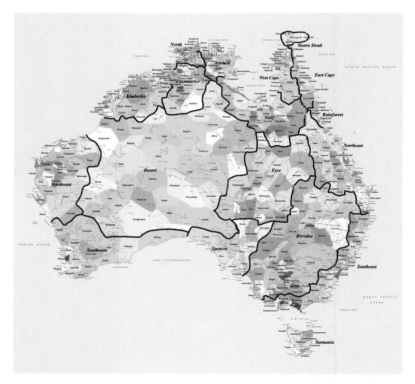

Aboriginal Australia language map.

Today, it is possible to find older people who are able to speak and understand more than one Indigenous language, Kriol, as well as English. Indigenous Australians are among the nation's most skilled users of language.

Language experts have shown that the languages spoken in the Torres Strait were influenced by both Melanesian and Aboriginal languages. Meriam Mir (which developed from Papuan languages) is spoken in the eastern Torres Strait, while Kala Lagaw Ya is spoken on the western, central and northern islands. In both cases, individual dialects are found on each of the islands.

Kriol and Yumplatok

Kriol has emerged in northern Australia as a means of communication across our cultures and between English-speakers and us. While many people are unhappy that Kriol tends to be used instead of traditional languages, it has unified many Aboriginal people. There are two major creoles: one spoken in Queensland, the Northern Territory and the West Australian cattle-station belt (Kriol); and one spoken in the Torres Strait and Cape York (Torres Strait Creole).

Torres Strait Creole (also commonly known as Yumplatok or Brokan) has developed over time. Its origin is Pacific Island 'pidgin' sometimes called Bislama (*Biche-la-mar*) which became a lingua franca (a language used by speakers of different languages to allow them to communicate) between Pacific Island seamen, the Islanders and others. It also became the language spoken between Eastern and Western Islanders. On islands like Erub, Masig, Poruma (Coconut) and Warraberr, it is now the vernacular. For most Islanders, English may be their second or third language, largely used to write and converse with non-Indigenous people (see p. 69).

Aboriginal place names

The use of Aboriginal words as place names varies considerably throughout the continent. From Toowoomba to Borrooloola, Canberra to

USING ABORIGINAL WORDS

Words like *mulga* have come into English to mean not just one acacia species, but the bush in general. *Mallee* is probably a Wemba Wemba word. The name of the Victorian Moomba festival comes from the Kulin word *moom*, which means *backside*. People find this amusing but it more correctly refers to sitting down or camping, which is what happens at a celebration, corroborree or festival. All Australians are familiar with the word *corroboree* for an Aboriginal dance and song festival but few know it is a Dharug word meaning to dance. *Gibber*, the word for *stony plains*, is also a Dharug word meaning to dance, while many Australians call the small thorn that sticks into your foot in summer by a word from several New South Wales languages: *bindi-eye*. *Yabber* is used now to describe voluble talk and it comes from the Woiwurrung language.

Coonawarra, Werribee to Woollongong, Manjimup to Maningrida, the names evoke our heritage. Australian prime ministers have represented the electorates of Bennelong and Kooyong and two of Australia's premier sports venues — Brisbane's Woollongabba Oval (Gabba) and Geelong's Kardinia Park — have Indigenous names. Most Geelong people are unaware that the city itself was called *Jallang*, or *tongue of land*, by the Wathaurong people.

Australians are becoming more accustomed to referring to central Australia's most famous landmark, Ayers Rock, by its Aboriginal name, Uluru. In New South Wales, many original place names are being successfully revived. In Melbourne, the city's newest park has been named Birrarung Marr. There is a move to give Mount Kosciuszko, the nation's tallest mountain, dual Polish and Aboriginal names.

Language maintenance and revival

Even though some missionary groups were among the first to learn and record our languages, and made translations of the Bible into those

KAURNA WARRA PINTYANDI (KWP)

Kaurna, the original language of the Adelaide Plains, was documented by German missionaries in the mid-nineteenth century but there are no sound recordings.

Since 1990, efforts have been made to re-introduce the language, and Kaurna is now taught to relatively small numbers of students at all levels of education. It is also used in speeches of welcome, songs, names (places, programs, events, people and pets etc.), and has been incorporated into a number of public artworks. Artwork at the entrance to Adelaide's Festival Theatre includes the words *Yertarra padnima, taingiwiltanendadlu* 'When we walk the land, then we become strong', inspired by Kaurna Elder Lewis O'Brien.

The Kaurna Warra Pintyandi (KWP) group meets regularly to work on language projects and to address requests for names, translations and information about the Kaurna language. At the request of the Adelaide City Council, the world's first solar bus was named Tindo 'sun' and carries the number plate 'Tindo 1'.

Around 3000 to 3500 Kaurna words were documented in historical sources, including more than 100 words for new things, such as *nurlitti* 'key'. Using these same patterns, many new words, such as *warraityatti* 'telephone', *turraityatti* 'television' and *mukarndo* 'computer' have been added to the language. Expressions have also been developed for use in a range of situations, including the classroom, talking with babies, playing football, fishing and services at funerals.

languages, colonial authorities and Christian missionaries were rarely sympathetic when we tried to retain our languages and our culture. Some of us who were taken into the missions were severely punished for speaking traditional language and practising culture (see p. 93,100). Much of the richness of our languages was lost in these years but today cultural centres are striving to reverse that loss. It is a complex recovery, as some communities may contain several language groups and to teach all of them in schools is impossible. The maintenance

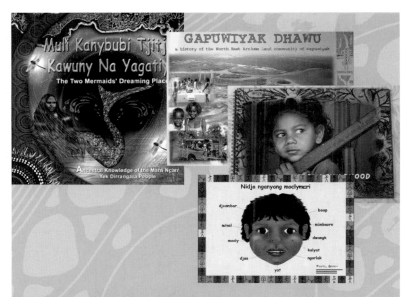

RETAINING OUR LANGUAGES

Many in our communities have a strong desire to publish our own materials in a way that respects our Indigenous Law, traditions and culture. Batchelor Press (part of the Batchelor Institute of Indigenous Tertiary Education) was created to meet this need and helps Indigenous Elders and educators satisfy common law needs as well as Indigenous communal rights.

The Press publishes Indigenous books, DVDs and CDs in our languages and English as requested by Elders and communities. It also publishes research reports and educational resources for Indigenous adults and the wider Australian community.

The content of our cultural and language publications is developed with community Elders and other community members, artists, storytellers and language workers, along with linguists, illustrators, editors and the publisher. The educational resources are produced with community members, students and teaching staff who have many years experience in bilingual education, ESL, curriculum development and distance learning for people in rural and remote communities.

and revival of languages are crucial to our cultural health. For many of us, our languages represent the keystone to our identities, Law and land claims.

In southern Australia we have revived many of our languages with the support of the Federation of Aboriginal and Torres Strait Island Languages (FATSIL) (see also p. 68–9).

We have worked with non-Indigenous language experts so we can record and keep our language and teach them to our children. Some communities are taking over the responsibility for updating and revitalising the use of their languages, sometimes involving the innovative use of technology.

People, Health and Homes

Population

Throughout two centuries since colonisation, but particularly in the past few decades, we have moved from remote and rural areas to large country towns and to more urban and metropolitan centres, particularly in the south-east of the country. Originally, this reflected the forced removals and dispossession from our lands. More recently, both Aboriginal and Torres Strait Islander people have moved in search of employment and better education.

Population loss and growth

While it can never be known for certain, some researchers estimate that the Indigenous population at the time of colonisation was 500 000 people. By 1933, after dispossession from our lands and with the effect of introduced diseases that came with the colonists, the experts estimate that our population was at its lowest point, at only 20 per cent of what it was in 1788. We were first counted as a discrete population in the national 1971 Census, and since then an increasing number of people have identified as Aboriginal and/or Torres Strait Islander. There was a 33 per cent increase between the 1991 and 1996 Censuses, and subsequently a 16 per cent increase between 1996 and 2001 and

Kids enjoy the afternoon at The Settlement, Darlington. L–R:
Curtley Kelly, Ben Kelly, Jay Williams, Kristian Kelly and Michael Kelly.

11 per cent between 2001 and 2006. This cannot be accounted for by
an increase in birth rate alone. The Australian Bureau of Statistics (ABS)
attributes the increases to the growing number of people who are self-
identifying as Indigenous, and to greater efforts being made to record
Indigeneity in the censuses. Identification as Indigenous is voluntary and
the ABS calculates 'experimental estimates' for the size of Indigenous
populations. They estimate that in 2006 there were 517 174 Indigenous
people, representing 2.5 per cent of the total population. Because some
of our population are mobile, it can be difficult to obtain accurate data.
Inaccurate data collection leads to an inadequate provision of services
like housing and health.

Generally, we have a much younger population age structure than
non-Indigenous Australians with high levels of fertility and mortality,
and with a median age of 20 years compared to 36.

Distribution of the Indigenous population across Australia, ABS data, 2006.

Remote, regional and city living

We make up most of the population in Australia's remote areas, from Torres Strait through to the desert regions of Western Australia, and a significant population in other outback areas, especially those distant from the larger towns. In Arnhem Land, for instance, we are 91 per cent of the population. In the south-east of the country, with its larger populations, we comprise only a small part of the total population. Over the decades, some regional areas were cleared for agriculture and not many of us remain living there. In the areas where the missions and reserves were set up, there are more of us. Although just over half of our total population lives in two states, New South Wales and Queensland, they make up only a small proportion of the overall populations of these states.

About 86 per cent of Torres Strait Islanders now live on the Australian mainland, mostly in urban centres along the coast of Queensland and New South Wales. Cairns and Townsville have lively Torres Strait Islander communities.

Artists Eileen Napaltjarri and Pantjiya Nungurrayi with Sharon Napurrula and a young boy in Kintore.

Back to Country

In 1976 the Australian government passed the Aboriginal Land Rights (Northern Territory) Act. In a move back to country, many people left the northern towns and mission settlements in the 1970s and established outstations on ancestral lands. Here our culture could be maintained without the distractions and conflicts of modern town life. Today, over 12 000 people live on more than 1000 outstations.

The Kuninjku people of western Arnhem Land have several outstations that have become increasingly prosperous. They sell artworks, work part time in tourism and environmental management projects as well as harvest food in the traditional way. The outstations have had a positive effect on the country as a result of traditional land care, and the transfer of cultural knowledge from old to young help sustain Kuninjku culture. Government policies encouraging self-determination — our ability to make decisions about what is done in our community — have assisted these communities.

In March 2008, the *Medical Journal of Australia* reported that the Alyawarr and Anmatjerr people on the sixteen outstations of Utopia, 290 kilometres north-east of Alice Springs, have a mortality rate almost half that of other Northern Territory Aboriginal peoples. The report explained why they live longer: they exercise more, eat a considerable amount of traditional food and have medical services that actively work to prevent disease.

While many of us live urban lives and are employed alongside other Australians, some groups have been able to continue traditional or semi-traditional lifestyles. Yet we are no less Aboriginal or Torres Strait Islander if we live in towns or cities. Many who are city dwellers return to our communities for times of ceremony and family business. We have successful doctors, lawyers, politicians, businesspeople, teachers, scientists, artists, environmentalists and sportspeople. Those of us who retain links with our ancestral country try to return, sustained by our culture, our kin and the spirit of our ancestors.

Health

We are less healthy than other Australians, and our continuing poor health cannot be understood solely in medical terms. The illnesses and their rates of occurrence require an understanding of the history of dispossession, colonisation, failed attempts at assimilation, racism and the denial of citizenship rights. There are two ways to consider our health. One is from a medical perspective (including comparisons with other countries). The other takes account of people's behaviour and recognises the things in society that affect health and wellbeing.

Statistics on life expectancy, infant mortality and birthweight are often used to describe the difference between people's health. Experts estimate that we live 17 years fewer than do non-Indigenous people, while our infant mortality rate is two to three times higher. Between 2001 and 2004, 13 per cent of our live-born babies were of low birthweight (less than 2500 grams) compared with 6 per cent for the rest of the population.

Those of us who live in the Northern Territory and Western Australia have significantly improved our life expectancy and infant mortality from the 1970s to the 1980s, but the figures for other Australians have also improved, so the gap has not narrowed. The Indigenous peoples of New Zealand, Canada and the USA, countries with similar colonial histories to Australia, also suffer worse health than their non-aboriginal

HELPING 'MOTHER TERESA'

Young Aboriginal woman Bec is a recent graduate of the Gugan Gulwan Youth Aboriginal Corporation's Numeracy and Literacy Program. Based in Canberra, the program runs two days a week for young disadvantaged Aboriginal and Torres Strait Islander people.

By the time Bec was thirteen years old, her life was out of control. She was drinking heavily and using drugs regularly. She ran away from home often. She had trouble participating in the classroom; anxiety and depression often left her feeling breathless. She skipped school after being bullied, bashed and isolated from her peers.

Bec's mother Robyn believes that the Gugan Gulwan program saved her daughter from the ACT Quamby Youth Detention Centre, or worse.

Five years later, Bec now cares about herself, her mum, and her 'family' at Gugan Gulwan. She has been called 'Mother Teresa' for her caring ways — her empathy, good heart, and dedication towards helping others — by trying to engage with other young people who also used the program.

Bec now has a full-time job. She dreams of being a teacher and hopes one day to work at Cherbourg Community School in Queensland.

Staff and workers with the Gugan Gulwan program feel richly rewarded having helped Bec save her life, and connect with and motivate others.

Bec is now a role model, and a potential mentor for other young Indigenous people at risk who may one day feel safe enough to realise their own dreams.

people, but Australia has the highest differences in life expectancy and infant mortality.

Heart attack, angina and stroke (diseases of the circulatory system) were the main causes (27 per cent) of early deaths between 2001 and 2005. Accidents, suicide and assault caused 17 per cent of deaths. Diabetes and other endocrine, nutritional and metabolic diseases were responsible for 12 per cent of deaths. Influenza, pneumonia, asthma, bronchitis and emphysema (respiratory diseases) and cancer were the next major causes of death.

Aspects of society such as education, housing, employment, income, poverty, law and justice, environment, social and emotional wellbeing, community development, racism and the ability to make good decisions for a community affect the health of all Australians. The aspects of society that affect us in particular are culture, special relationship to land, a history of dispossession and our unique forms of organisation.

Joyce Dimer, Community Health Team leader at the South-West Aboriginal Medical Service, hosting a breast screening day for community members.

Norma Griffen is a qualified dental assistant at Durri where she underwent her training and where she has been employed for the past 18 years.

DURRI ABORIGINAL CORPORATION MEDICAL SERVICE

Durri began more than twenty-five years ago in a small building in the Green Hills Aboriginal community in an Aboriginal reserve outside Kempsey, northern New South Wales. 'Durri' means 'meeting of many rivers' in the Dungutti Nations language. Now located in downtown Kempsey, it provides best practice in several program areas: dental therapy, diabetes, immunisation and antenatal care. The organisation prides itself on offering equal access to all local and family groups: 'Our goal is to make primary health care and education accessible to all members of the community in a culturally appropriate and spiritually sensitive manner.' That long-serving staff at the dental clinic now treat a second generation of patients affirms that preventive treatment and education are working well and that patients have confidence in the staff and service.

For Australia to move forward as a caring society, the gap between our health and that of other Australians needs to be closed, which will mean working on both the medical and social causes. Aboriginal community-controlled health services — more than 140 of them throughout Australia — are an essential part of this solution. In December 2007, the Council of Australian Governments (COAG) committed itself to closing the 17-year gap in life expectancy, but more can, and needs, to be done.

Housing

In warm areas, bark and timber shelters were more than adequate in most seasons but across the country we took advantage of natural caves for permanent shelter and built a range of shelters with stone, timber, turf or foliage.

In many ways our traditional forms of shelter were much better suited to the landscape and climate than some of the colonial architecture based on designs for the colder climate of the northern hemisphere.

Traditional Island dwellings in the Torres Strait were strong, with either a bamboo or mangrove framework and poles, and thatched roofs and walls made of palm leaves and grass. Those in the north were built on poles above the ground; those in the east were shaped like beehives.

In north-west Tasmania people scooped out the soil so they and their fires could be below ground level, and built strong beehive dwellings above, plastered with mud. Some fitted a family, others allowed for

An outstation residence at Puntawari in the Little Sandy Desert, Western Australia, 1991. Lack of funds resulted in a combination of traditional bush materials and portable low-cost Western materials.

A typical island hut on Mer (Murray Island) in the Torres Strait. This was was built by Eddie Koiki Mabo.

people to get together. At Lake Condah and nearby in western Victoria, people built seasonally inhabited villages of stone dwellings with timber roofs.

Diaries and official colonial records report the existence of more substantial Indigenous housing in western Victoria, but over most of the continent, our mobile adaptation meant that it was not worth the investment in time and energy to build substantial dwellings.

Culture and Sport

Our traditions have been assaulted by the cultures of the waves of people who have come to our country. However, many have survived even in those parts of southern and eastern Australia where colonial impacts were longest and strongest. They continue to evolve in defiance of the expectation that we would simply merge with the dominant culture.

Traditional stories, regional differences

In the north of the country, our traditional stories, generally speaking, are strong and are retold in ceremony for both Indigenous and non-Indigenous Australians. There are many Dreamings and stories for all regions, but on the Larapinta Trail near Alice Springs, for example, visitors can't help but be aware of the Caterpillar Dreaming. In Arnhem Land the Yolngu record their interaction with Macassan traders with the Red Flag dance. The Titjikala community, south of Alice Springs, tell the story of the evil Itikiwarra, the knob-tailed gecko spirit ancestor, while the Anangu of northern South Australia have the Kuniya songline, where the woman python lays her eggs on a slab of rock, leaving landmarks across the country.

It is important to remember that southern Indigenous people have retained significant elements of their culture and are reclaiming more. At Gariwerd (in The Grampians) in Victoria, the traditional story of the stars of the Southern Cross is told in both traditional dance and contemporary film. Further north, Torres Strait Islanders give a rich meaning to the constellation when they talk about the story of the warrior Tagai (see p. 13).

While cultures and traditions across the country have much in common there are distinct regional differences. In the Torres Strait, many of our dances and songs refer to the local environment, while others reveal contact and influences from as far away as the South Sea Islands.

Dancers of all ages participate in the daily bunggul at the annual Garma Festival of Traditional Culture.

Our contemporary art, music and dance declare that we are proud of our identity, and that our sustaining special relationship with our lands, our islands and the seas has survived with us.

The Arts

The energies of our artists and excitement about their work are recognised worldwide as among Australia's most distinctive cultural contributions. Our contemporary forms of art and performance express our unique world views and reflect our engagement with ever-growing audiences. Some of these views come from hundreds of generations of veneration of the ancestral creation of the land while others provide critical new perspectives on Australia's colonial experience.

Music

Traditional Aboriginal music is a vocal art — we sing — and songs may often be 'given' to singers by a Dreaming being, most commonly during dreams. A series of these songs, which may have many verses, tells a story of a Dreaming ancestor who sang as they travelled through the land. These songs are passed down from generation to generation and can help people live well on their land by describing water sources or places where plants or game are plentiful. People who own the songs are the traditional owners of the land. Ownership of the songs is proof of continuous association, an important requirement for land claims.

The popular band Yothu Yindi, from north-east Arnhem Land, uses traditional Yolngu melodies and words in its songs, while, in 'Brown-Skinned Baby', Bob Randall follows an earlier practice of shaming people by describing a tragic situation. Singers in New South Wales used to do this to shame people who cheated at two-up games. Jimmy Little, from Cummeragunga on the Murray River in New South Wales, sang 'Royal Telephone' on TV in the 1960s and launched a long and illustrious career, inspired by his parents. Many of our communities were sustained by songs like 'Nemeralla Pines', 'Yorta Yorta Man' and others that protested against the conditions faced by Aboriginal people.

Recording the didjeridu with songmen at Wadeye, July 1999. L–R: John Nummar, Charles Kungiung, Maurice Ngulkur, Les Kundjil, Allan Marett and Ambrose Miarlum.

Kev Carmody's 'From Little Things Big Things Grow' (co-written with Paul Kelly) might be a contemporary classic of popular modern music, but it has evolved directly from the Aboriginal country-and-western music common on pastoral stations and in rural areas. Similarly, Archie Roach sang of 'Charcoal Lane' in inner-city Melbourne's Fitzroy but the lament has its basis in the mission settlements of Framlingham and Lake Condah in country Victoria where he lived.

Troy Cassar-Daley, Ruby Hunter, Kutcha Edwards, the Stiff Gins and many others are successful in the field of popular music. Cairns-born Torres Strait Islander, Christine Anu originally trained as a dancer. Her debut album, *StylinUp*, included her version of 'My Island Home', which later won an award for songwriter Neil Murray. In a different field,

DIDJ MUSIC

The didgeridoo (called the *yidaki* in Arnhem Land in the Northern Territory) is a wind instrument used by many people. It is perhaps our best-known musical instrument, which is made from the hollow limb or trunk of a tree and decorated with traditional designs.

The didgeridoo produces a range of resonant sounds as the player moves lips, tongue and throat while simultaneously breathing through the nose and out through the instrument to maintain a consistent sound. It can be made in different keys and is played alongside clapping sticks and skin drums that provide the rhythm and beat for dancers.

William Barton was taught the didgeridoo by his uncle, an elder of the Wannyi, Lardil and Kalkadunga tribes of western Queensland. Well-known to concert-goers in Australia and overseas, his 2005 collaboration with Sean O'Boyle, *Concerto for Didgeridoo*, is a unique blend of ancient music tradition and a Western classical music art-form.

William has played with symphony orchestras all over the world, and collaborated memorably with Tyrone Noonan in Oxfam's Closing the Gap Day: a major national effort to end the health crisis facing Indigenous Australians.

Maroochy Barambah and Deborah Cheetham have became celebrated performers of Western classical music, following in the footsteps of the famous singer, Harold Blair (1924–76).

The Warumpi Band, which takes its name from the Honey Ant Dreaming site near Papunya in the Northern Territory, developed a unique style of rock music. In 1983, the band members wrote, recorded and released the first rock song in an Aboriginal language, 'Jailanguru Pakarnu' ('Out of Jail'). It was voted one of the top ten recordings in the National Film and Sound Archive's listings, Sounds of Australia, in 2007.

Younger members of our community are drawing on musical influences from overseas and adapting them for their own purposes. While it emerged from the urban slums of the USA, hip hop has found a new home in neglected outback communities and in the cities. The Wilcannia Mob, aged just ten- to thirteen-years-old, won a Deadly Award ('deadly' means excellent or desirable) with their song 'Down River', which draws on their Barkanji River heritage. It was recorded in a lounge room and went on to the Top 100 on the Australian Broadcasting Commission's (ABC) Triple J radio station. Aboriginal hip hop is a popular way for young men and women to build on our oral culture heritage. Tjimba and the Yung Warriors are experiencing success with their adaptation of this form, appealing directly to young people while still celebrating their Indigenous roots.

Torres Strait Islanders have always been skilled absorbers and adaptors of the musical traditions of other people. By the end of 1872, one year after the London Missionary Society had arrived, hymns and choruses were sung each day. In the early twentieth century, influential Anglo-American musical forms spread through the Strait and met the Indigenous music of the islands, which was being transformed by the sacred music of the South Sea Islander missionaries.

In the 1950s, Torres Strait Island music developed in another direction when the late Solkos Tabo, Weser Whaleboat, Sonny Kadcy and George Passi began composing songs in the style of Hawaiian-Par-Pacific songs which became the music for 'hula' concerts. At the same time, Thursday

Islanders Seaman Dan and George Dewis were learning the songs of Nat King Cole and others. Competition between Islander composers was strong and the songs later became known as Kole Kabem Wed and replaced European music in the islands' dancehalls. Rock'n'roll arrived in the Torres Strait in the late 1960s with band leaders like Ritti Doolah.

There are songs for all pastimes, from playing to boating and songs to accompany sacred and secular dances. Traditionally, few musical instruments were used apart from the human voice and drums. Occasionally, percussion was added, a rattle, with jew's harps, pan pipes and notched flutes providing the wind instruments. Today, these have been replaced by other instruments.

With the coming of local radio and, later, TV, the unique Torres Strait Islander musical culture is less dominant than it used to be, though most of the music heard in the islands until the 1990s was locally composed. This music is still maintained in a lively way among the older generation and in the large groups of people who have moved away from the islands.

The Mills Sisters adopted church and popular music from their home islands to become successful performers throughout Australia, while singer Rita Mills has toured the world, sharing her Torres Strait culture and music.

Theatre and dance

Dance is a vital expression of traditional Aboriginal culture as a whole, as part of ceremonies or as entertainment. Body painting and a variety of paraphernalia, including head-dresses, are associated with dance.

Many traditional dances depict incidents from activities of the creative beings in the Dreaming era. Other dances tell stories about the land and the community and their relationships. Different communities tell their own stories; each group has its own distinct style of expression, and in some areas families pass down dances from one generation to the next. The best dancers are held in high esteem by the community.

Thursday Island's Henry 'Seaman' Dan with grandson
Patrick Mau on the cover of a hip-hop single they
recorded together.

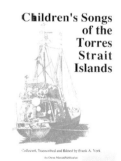

'Children's Songs
of the Torres
Strait' title page,
by Frank York.

Bangarra Dance Company perform 'Corroboree' in
Sydney 2001.

Some dances have their origins in the past, while others are more
contemporary. The Aeroplane Dance tells the story of a World War II
bomber that came down near Borroloola in the Northern Territory.
Dancers mimic the flight of the aeroplane while performing the
traditional stamping dance.

A recent adaptation of non-Indigenous dance is by the Chooky
Dancers, whose 'Zorba the Greek Yolngu Style' has become a hit on
YouTube. While they originally devised the dance just for fun, the
young men have now been invited to perform around Australia and
internationally.

The Bangarra Dance Theatre is a leading modern Australian dance
company that is forging an international reputation for artistic innovation.
Stephen Page is the company's artistic director. The source of Bangarra's

inspiration is Indigenous culture and each of the members in the group draws on the culture of their own heritage. The Saibai Dancers are the best in the Torres Strait, especially known for bow-and-arrow dances.

The theatre production *Bran Nue Day* and its music are true to the heart of the Broome area. Jimmy Chi and the Figram Brothers have toured this very popular production throughout Australia; Chi's *Corrugation Road* has also been performed in many Australian cities.

Sydney and other major city audiences had the chance to learn Pitjantjatjara when they went to the theatre to see *Ngapartji Ngapartji* ('I give you something; you give me something'), which describes the Spinifex people's encounter with weapons testing at Woomera (1953 to 1965) in remote South Australia.

A vast world audience was introduced to Indigenous performers at the opening of the 2000 Olympic Games in Sydney, where athlete Cathy Freeman — an Indigenous performer of another kind — lit the Olympic cauldron.

Torres Strait Islanders adopted other influences in dance as well as music. The *Taibobo*, songs and dances from the South Sea Island people, were taught to every Islander. Torres Strait Islanders soon began to compose their own *Taibobo*. Contemporary Island dance songs, *Segur Kab Wed*, date back to between 1900 and 1910. In the 1920s, in a mere two weeks, some of the best dancers from Badu, Moa, Yam and Murray Islands combined the traditional *Kab-Kar* and the newer *Taibobo* into one dance. This happened when a group of pearling luggers sailed to Mabuiag Island, and the men held a dance workshop while seeking shelter from bad weather. *Play Song* became part of that dance and it is now known widely in North Queensland and Papua as *Segur Kaba Wed*, meaning 'play dance and song'.

Gail Mabo, the artistic director of the Mabo Company, is the daughter of Eddie Koiki Mabo, whose fame arose from the struggle for native title (see p. 116). The dance and theatre performance is inspired by her father's knowledge and passion for his beliefs, and uses traditional implements, musical instruments and historical footage. The Mabo Company dancers come from Cairns, Townsville and the Torres Strait.

Gail Mabo, The Mabo Dance Company director, with dancer, Albert David.

Art

We have always been artists. We paint in rock shelters and caves, on our bodies for ceremony and in some regions we construct vast artworks on the ground as vital components of ritual. Rock painting from the Kimberley's Carpenter's Gap has been dated to 40 000 years ago and the concentric circle art of central Australia is thought to be the oldest continuing art tradition in the world. We also paint on tools, shields and musical instruments.

Internationally renowned artist, John Mawundjul, painting at Milmilngkan near Manirgrida, Northern Territory, © Luke Taylor

Our artists make art for sale and the styles are as diverse as the cultures and histories of the artists. They draw on ceremonial arts in order to teach outsiders about our religion. The Aboriginal art movement at Papunya Tula grew out of ceremonial designs made on the ground but now the artists paint huge canvasses for museums and galleries around the world. In Arnhem Land, intricate body-art ochre designs are now also painted on large pieces of flat bark, which are offered for sale, and many of which now hang in art galleries.

Emily Kame Kngwarreye and Kathleen Petyarre of Utopia, Clifford Possum Tjapaltjarri of Papunya, Rover Thomas of Warmun and Banduk Marika of Yirrkala are internationally well known: all are artists who participated in ceremony and used that experience as inspiration in their creation of contemporary art.

Hermannsburg, where the famous painter Albert Namatjira first worked (see p. 108), is nowadays also a major location for women's decorated ceramics.

Yvonne Koolmatrie lives in the Riverland region and makes innovative sculptures and traditional fishtrap forms in fibre with coil-weaving techniques learnt from Shirley Trevorrow. At Ernabella, Jillian Davey and others work in new techniques of batik and print-making, and the colours and designs relate to their experience of a unique landscape.

Others have drawn on their urban experiences to create art in new formats that include photography and film, as well as sculpture, jewellery and painting in new materials. Waanyi artist Judy Watson's etched zinc panels are celebrated in many public buildings in Australian cities. Photographer Michael Riley grew up in Dubbo and was a founding member of the Boomalli Aboriginal Artists Cooperative in Sydney. Victorian Aboriginal artists Vicki Couzens, Treahna Hamm and Lee Darroch have revived the art of decorating possum-skin cloaks.

Tasmanian artists like Dulcie Greeno, Patsy Cameron and Lola Greeno are teaching shell necklace-making, basketry and working with kelp to a younger generation of artists. Torres Strait Islander Denis Nona, from Badu Island, was taught traditional woodcarving techniques that he translated into intricate linocuts. He has also been encouraged to interpret creation stories in bronze sculptures, and he and Alick Tipoti's art is now exhibited internationally. Ken Thaiday Snr, a Torres Strait Islander artist living on the mainland, has developed elaborate headdress sculptures based on the themes of traditional dances. Richard Bell and Destiny Deacon provide acidic comment on issues of sexism, racism, and the place of Aboriginal arts in contemporary Australia in their images and installations. Our artists' work is often sold through our own community organisations. We also license our art to others and

Vicki Couzens in a new possum skin cloak, in front of her painting, *woorrkgnan — moorraka (birthplace — burial place)* representing one of the last traditional cloaks.

BUYING OUR ART

These days our art is leading the way in Australian art sales. Buyers may be attracted by its investment potential or they might be drawn to our artists' unique connections with country that are celebrated in the art. Major auction houses have many sales throughout the year and the prices for some now deceased artists are skyrocketing. Unlike France, Australia does not yet have a law that requires some of the resale profit to be returned to our artists' families. For our artists, money from the sale of art is extremely important income, especially in very remote locations where there are few other job opportunities. Across Australia there is a network of community-based Aboriginal and Torres Strait Islander arts centres that help to promote and guarantee the authenticity of the work they sell. The arts centres also organise exhibitions with reputable dealers in southern cities. Potential buyers can teach themselves about the major art centres by learning from the informative catalogues sold at state and national art galleries and museums.

the images we produce can be found on a range of clothes and other objects.

Each year our Indigenous talent in the arts and sport is celebrated at the Deadly Awards and the Red Ochre Awards. Originally as a celebration for our own communities, these events are fast making their mark on the wider arts scene, while the annual Telstra National Aboriginal and Torres Strait Islander Art Award is both a competition and a celebration of our art and culture. Those responsible for Indigerous art in the galleries of capital cities around the country regularly organise large exhibitions featuring a range of art forms.

Our flags

We are proud of our identity as Indigenous people and our flags are a widely recognised symbol of it. When Cathy Freeman wrapped herself in the Aboriginal flag after her win in the 1994 Commonwealth Games, most Australians embraced her right to do so and did not see it as a threat to the nation, though her gesture attracted criticism. Many regional councils, schools and individuals are proud to fly both the Australian national flag and the Aboriginal and/or the Torres Strait Island flag in recognition of the country's history and shared future.

The Aboriginal flag was designed by Harold Thomas, an Arrernte man from central Australia and was first flown on National Aboriginal Day in July 1971 in Adelaide. It was given legal recognition in July 1995 as a flag of Australia. It has bands of black and red with a central yellow sun. The red at the bottom represents the Earth and our relationship to it. The black above represents all the Aboriginal people including our ancestors. The yellow sun is, of course, the source of life.

The Torres Strait Islander flag was designed by Bernard Namok from Thursday Island. It was first flown in 1992 and was given legal recognition in July 1995 as a flag of Australia. It has horizontal bands, two of green for the land and one of blue for the sea. The bands are separated by black lines representing the people. The white *dari/dhoeri* is a traditional headdress and represents our culture while the five-pointed white star represents the five island groups: eastern, western, central, and the areas surrounding Port Kennedy and inhabited islands

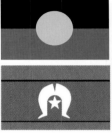

The Aboriginal and Torres Strait Islander flags, recognised under federal legislation in 1995.

Harold Chatfield of Winnunga Nimmityjah Aboriginal Health Services and his son Carney holding the two flags, NAIDOC Day, Canberra 2007.

the northern peninsula. Originally made from bird feathers, *dari/dhoeri* are now made from a range of materials.

Film and television

Our artists readily adapt to new media, and TV and cinema have become home to some of our celebrated artists. Deborah Mailman, Leah Purcell, David Gulpilil, Ernie Dingo, Luke Carroll and Aaron Pederson appear regularly on our cinema and TV screens. Chef and film-maker Mark Olive has brought our cuisine to national attention through his cooking demonstrations for the ABC's *Message Stick* and the Lifestyle Channel. Films like *Radiance* (Rachel Perkins), *Beneath Clouds* (Ivan Sen) and *Harry's War* (Richard Frankland) have provided insider visions of Aboriginal and Torres Strait Islander lives to mainstream audiences in contemporary cinema. Frances Peters-Little, a Kamilaroi–Uralari film-maker and academic, won a Sundance Award for her film *Tent Embassy* and has produced documentaries for the ABC. Richard Frankland has also made documentaries, and his 2007 film *Convincing Ground* explored the legal battle by Gunditjmara people to prevent development on a massacre site at Portland in Victoria. Steve Kinnane co-wrote the award-winning documentary *The Coolbaroo Club*, which highlighted the conditions we experienced in Perth in the 1950s and 1960s that were virtually the same as the officially segregated apartheid conditions in South Africa. The television series *Remote Area Nurse* was filmed on Masig Island in the Torres Strait and gave viewers insights into

On set of 'One Night the Moon' in Adnyamathanha Country (aka Flinders Ranges) written and directed by Rachel Perkins (centre).

the work of nursing in remote communities as well as the contemporary lives of Torres Strait Islanders.

The national Tudawali Awards, which celebrate the achievements of those of us working in the film, video and TV industry, are named after Robert Tudawali, a man of Tiwi Island descent who was brought up on Melville Island in the Northern Territory. Known best for playing the male lead role in the film *Jedda*, he followed this with other film roles. In 1965 he worked at Wave Hill Station as a stockman and became a spokesperson for the Gurindji strikers (see p. 109).

Writers

Like our film-makers and artists, our writers have embraced and now excel in a non-traditional artform. Alexis Wright, Melissa Lucashenko, Anita Heiss, Terri Janke, Vivienne Cleven, Jared Thomas, Samuel Wagan Watson, Philip McLaren, Tony Birch and John Clarke are just some of our authors who write in English using the most modern literary styles, especially in fiction and poetry. Two of our authors, Kim Scott (*Benang*) and Alexis Wright (*Carpentaria*), have won the Miles Franklin Award, Australia's most prestigious writing prize. Some of our writers leave us in no doubt that their stories are unique and evolved from the traditional storytelling of this country. *Carpentaria* was written by Wright in the style of traditional storytelling and myth. It is an epic work that captures and celebrates the country, culture and political battles of her people. These writers draw on the literary heritage provided by acclaimed literary forebears like Jack Davis, Kevin Gilbert and Oodgeroo Noonuccal. Like Kim Scott's *Benang*, Steve Kinnane's *Shadow Lines* uses West Australian government and police records to plot the course of Australia's assimilationist approach, which assumed our cultures would die out and we would simply blend into the culture of the colonisers.

Our writers now appear at literary festivals and events around the country, talking about their own work and Indigenous literature, as well as taking part in mainstream sessions.

Author, Anita Heiss, addressing the audience at Wordstorm writers' festival, Darwin 2005

Today we have acclaimed writers working in many areas of literature. For example, Martin Nakata and Lester-Irabinna Rigney write books for tertiary education. The *Indij Readers For Big Fullas and Little Fullas* series of children's books, were created to foster and increase children's literacy in the primary education system. North Queensland's Black Ink Press produce a range of children's books, some of which have been used in the accelerated literacy program in the Northern Territory and Western Australia. We have our own publishing houses, too, including Magabala Books in Broome, the Institute of Aboriginal Development (IAD) in Alice Springs, Batchelor Press in Katherine (see p. 27) and Aboriginal Studies Press (part of AIATSIS) in Canberra.

We began writing soon after the colonisers introduced this form of communication to the country. From the early days of the colonies, we adopted and used it for our own ends. Bennelong's letter of 1796 was dictated to a scribe, but soon after we took printed objects and written papers beyond the frontiers of colonisation. Some were assimilated into our graphics and social life, and by the 1830s and 1940s the Palawa people of Tasmania, among others, were creating subversive versions of the Bible, as well as writing sermons, community newspapers and letters to colonial authorities. For example, people from Lake Condah and Corranderk in Victoria wrote letters to the government complaining of conditions on the missions. These letters and others are part of a resistance to white control of our lives that has endured.

Copy of a letter from a Native of Botany Bay (to Mr Phillips, Lord Sydney's steward) being returned to his own country after he had resided a short time in England.

Sidney Cove
New S. Wales Aug.st 29
1796

Sir
I am very well. I hope you are very well. I live at the Governor's. I have every day dinner there. I have not my wife: another black man took her away: we have had murry* doings: he spear'd me in the back, but I better now: his name is now ×t Carroway. all my friends alive & well. not me go to England no more. I am at home now. I hope Sir you send me anything you please Sir. hope all are well in England. I hope Mr. Phillip very well. You nurse me Madam when I sick. you very good Madam: thank you Madam, & hope you remember me Madam, not forget. I know you very well Madam. Madam I want Stockings. thank you Madam; send me two pair stockings. you very good Madam. Thank you Madam. Sir, you give my duty to Ld Sydney. Thank you very good my Lord. very good: hope very well all family. very well. Sir, send me you please some Handkerchiefs for Pocket. you please Sir send me some shoes: two pair you please Sir.

Bannolong

× meaning bad.   ×t they frequently change their names

The handwritten copy of Bennelong's original letter, written 29 August 1796.

WORKING WITH INDIGENOUS WRITERS

Collaborations between Indigenous creators and non-Indigenous counterparts are becoming common and in this way some amazing stories can be shared with a large audience. To avoid problems, issues relating to copyright and royalty payments need to be decided early. One solution is for the Indigenous creator to retain copyright (*story as told to [name of] non-Indigenous author*), or it can be shared between the two creators. The likely income and the share of royalties should be explained in advance too. Royalties from publications will be very different from the mining royalties a community might receive.

Editors working on Aboriginal texts and images should understand that the material derives from an Indigenous consciousness. It's tied to family, land (knowledge of past and present), language group, traditional wellbeing, contemporary spirituality, and the links that bind all of these to country. Aboriginal people may speak as if country is a living and breathing entity, with emotions and consciousness.

Creators' quirky phrases and outlooks should be retained as they add to the richness that is their life and creation. Certain words can be loaded with symbolism and deeply embedded in culture, and editors need to understand this.

Editors should check material relating to law and culture with the appropriate community people, letting them know how the material will be used and where the books might be sold. They should also resolve how the family want to deal with the naming of deceased people (text or images). Where necessary, a warning should be placed at the beginning of the publication.

A valuable tool for readers editors might want to include is an orthography, where written or printed symbols represent the sounds of a language.

Media

Indigenous newspapers, notably the *Koori Mail*, the *National Indigenous Times* and the *Torres News*, play a pivotal role in communicating Aboriginal and Torres Strait Island culture, politics and sport, as do radio programs like the ABC's *Message Stick*, *Speaking Out*, *Awaye!* and SBS TV's *Living Black*.

We now frequently work through the Central Australian-based Central Australia Aboriginal Media Association, which has TV and radio broadcasting, an independent music label and film and TV production. Imparja is a commercial service in remote areas that broadcasts radio and TV programs via satellite across more than 4.5 million square kilometres. National Indigenous Television (NITV) is a new 24-hour service that aims to inform, entertain and educate, preserve our languages, tell our stories and showcase the rich diversity of our cultures and creative talent.

Gavin Jones, *Deadly Vibe* magazine's editor-in-chief, with actor Luke Carroll at the launch of NITV, 2007.

Former dancer and now comedian, Sean Choolburra

OUR COMEDIANS

We are renowned for our humour. Anyone who saw the film *Ten Canoes* will agree. Our oral culture gives us great skills in telling stories and jokes. The TV series *Bush Mechanics* revealed the good humour and ingenuity of a group of young men from the remote Warlpiri community of Yuendumu, whose inventive use of available resources keeps their vehicles moving.

Sean Choolburra from Townsville won the Raw Comedy 2002 state final. Sean also plays the didgeridoo, sings, dances, acts and writes songs. Leah Purcell, from Murgon in south-west Queensland, received no formal acting training but co-wrote and performed the play *Box the Pony*, which was her creative idea, as well as acting on film and stage and writing the book *Black Chicks Talking*. In the West, Mary G (Mark Bin Bakar) has become a comedy phenomenon. His 'Queen of the Kimberley' has become a voice for Indigenous women with some audiences still struggling to believe Mary G is actually a man. Mark works to create business opportunities for Aboriginal artists and musicians and to help the cultural, health and educational development of communities.

Our writers, artists and musicians often combine their art with service to their community and, although this means less time for creative work, their connections to family and community are crucial ingredients of their performance.

Sport

Success in sport has inspired young Aboriginal and Torres Strait Islander people and has often provided opportunities for us to pursue success on an equal basis with other Australians. Younger people revere our champions and aspire to be like them. In many remote communities, kicking a football around is often the only game in town. Australian Football League (AFL) player Adam Goodes thinks that 'when Aborigines play Australian football with a clear mind and total focus, [it is as if] we are born to play it'.

Aboriginal men playing a game which some believe to be the precursor to AFL. Others dispute the idea.

SPORTSMEN TOUR OVERSEAS

While the reputations of our current athletes are known to many, few people know that Australia's first sports group to tour overseas was a team of Aboriginal cricketers. They had been taught cricket by pastoralists in western Victoria's Lake Wallace region. That they toured at all is surprising. Despite racism, rigid control of their lives from the missions and rumoured exploitation and illness, the players arrived in England in May 1868. They had 14 wins, 14 losses and 19 draws. One player, King Cole, died on tour and two players, Sundown and Jim Crow, were sent home, ill. It was to be the last such tour. A year after their return the *Aborigines Protection Act 1869* came into being. Had it come into force twelve months earlier, the team would not have toured because of concerns for their well-being.

Bullocky (traditional name: Bullchanach), the wicketkeeper-batsman for the Australian Aboriginal cricket team tour of England in 1868.

We have always played sport. Some games were played by men, women and children. The balls that were used in throwing and kicking games were sometimes made from kangaroo or possum skin sewn tightly, and others from paperbark, tied with pandanus fibre twine, and even from emu feathers. In the Torres Strait, children played with balls woven from plaited pandanus or coconut leaf strips. We played games

SCORING IN THE USA

Torres Strait's Patrick Mills now plays for St Mary's College Gaels in California. In 2008 he won three awards at the prestigious Western Coast Conference (WCC) 2008 men's basketball competition in the USA. In announcing the awards, the WCC said Mills has had an immediate impact on Saint Mary's program.

This is the first time Mills has been away from home: 'I miss my family, friends and my Mum's cooking,' Mills said.

Australians have been keenly following the tall youngster because of his background.

Mills' parents, Benny, a Torres Strait Islander, and Yvonne, an Aboriginal woman, are well known in the Canberra community after starting the Shadows Basketball Club.

Young Indigenous people in particular look up to Mills: 'That's a big deal to me,' Mills says. 'I try to get the message out to the young Australian kids that they should give it a go and making the most of the opportunities.'

Before leaving for the USA Mills was named the 2006 Australia Basketball Player of the Year and was only the third Indigenous player to earn a spot on the national team. Mills was one of Australia's 2008 Olympic men's basketball team.

of football, a game like hockey using a ball and stick, bowling in South Australia and Victoria (like 'boules'), and made spinning balls and tops.

Many people are familiar with our remarkable sportspeople, especially in football codes, athletics and boxing, where they have excelled, although there are Aboriginal and Torres Strait Islander champions in just about every sport played in Australia.

OUR SOCCER CHAMPIONS

Aboriginal achievement in football — Australian Rules, Rugby League and Rugby Union — is well documented, but achievement in the 'world game', soccer (European 'football'), has been missed. Aboriginal players like Charles Perkins, John Moriarty, Gordon Briscoe and Harry Williams scaled the heights of achievement in Australian soccer. The multicultural environment of Australian soccer after World War II may have offered Aboriginal players a haven from the prejudice and racism of a wider Australian society. The soccer historian Sid Grant noted more than thirty years ago that Aboriginal players had 'excelled in the junior ranks, especially in the Northern Territory'.

Other football codes recognised and overcame the barriers that stopped young Indigenous players reaching their potential. They established connections with Indigenous communities and broke down barriers, establishing training and coaching programs that target Indigenous communities, with profitable returns. The late Johnny Warren had no hesitation in forcefully stating that in the past 'the authorities, including the Australia Soccer Federation, were negligent in seeing the potential that lies within Aboriginal communities not addressed'.

Despite the obstacles, there have been some outstanding and prominent Indigenous players, such as Jade North from Taree, New South Wales, who is a member of the Australian national football team and played in Australia's quarter-final effort at the Athens Olympic Games in 2004; and Travis Dodd from Adelaide, who played his debut international match at the Asian Cup against Kuwait in 2006. He scored the opening goal for the home side in a 2–0 win, marking the first ever international goal scored by an Indigenous Australian player.

Jade North, centre fullback for the Australian A-League
Club, Newcastle United Jets FC. He is also a member of the
Australian national football team.

Successful Indigenous sportspeople have been taken into the heart
and soul of Australia. Cathy Freeman at the Sydney Olympics, Michael
Long in the AFL, the Ella brothers and Wendell Sailor on rugby grounds
all over the world, Evonne Goolagong playing tennis at Wimbledon,
Lionel Rose and Anthony Mundine in the boxing ring, Patrick Johnson
in the sprints and Nova Peris representing Australia in both hockey and
track events at the Olympic Games — all have introduced Australians to
high-achieving Indigenous Australians.

Nancy Long, Cilla Preece, Maureen Mossman and Joy Savage from Wuchopperen Health Services, Queensland, Category B Winner, Indigenous Governance Awards, 2006.

Participation and Governance

Education

For tens of thousands of years our world view, spirituality and practical survival skills have been handed down to successive generations. But many of us understand that today, for our children to reach their potential, they need to complete their school education. More of our youth are completing Year 12 and going on to vocational or tertiary studies.

Bilingual education was used by missionaries in the Pitjantjatjara lands in northern South Australia in the 1940s. It spread to a few other communities and in the 1970s was introduced into Northern Territory remote government schools and a few schools in Northern Queensland and outback Western Australia. 'Bilingual education' refers to teaching people to read and write in their mother tongue or first language for the first few years and then switching to literacy and instruction in the national or mainstream language. In Australia, this is Standard Australian English. The reasoning behind this is that it is easier to learn to read and write in a second language if a person is literate in their first language.

Wreck Bay Aboriginal Corporation member and Australian National University trainee fire ecologist Darren Brown with a diamond python. Wreck Bay Aboriginal Community's strategies involve young people in looking after country.

Yolngu Taris
Ashley Wagilak
from Ramingining
Community Education
Centre, playing
literacy games on
the computer.

RAMINGINING COMMUNITY EDUCATION CENTRE

**Ramingining Community Education Centre in north-east Arnhem
Land teaches children from preschool to Year 12. At the community's
request, the teachers speak entirely in English.**

School council chair, Albert Waninymarr explains:

Yolngu education is being taught at home every day. A mainstream
English curriculum is taught at school because new Balanda [non-
Indigenous] skills are needed in communities all the time. Things are
changing and English education is needed. You need your English and
literacy in daily life. It wasn't the government's policy to say 'no' to a
bilingual school here. It was a Yolngu choice. Yolngu culture is being
practised every day at home. The kids won't lose that.

Students at Ramingining understand the decision:

I'm learning lots of English so I can get a job at Ramingining at school
to teach children or fix things. (Naomi Garrawurra, age 8)

It is important to come to school for learning. It is important to
speak English so Balanda people understand us. I need English for
everything. To get job. I want to get job in Melbourne. That is my
favourite place. (Dino Wanybarrnga, age 14)

**Yolngu staff assist teachers by providing a strong link between
teachers and families. Yolngu teaching staff are encouraged to
study for formal teaching qualifications at the Batchelor Institute of
Indigenous Tertiary Education, cementing their positions as future
teachers at the school.**

TALKING IN TONGUES

'It's the white kids and the black kids,' says Sharon Cooke, an Aboriginal education consultant, describing the teaching of Aboriginal language at St Joseph's Catholic School in Walgett, New South Wales. 'They all learn together and sing together, it's really quite beautiful, it's quite emotional when you see it ... and not just for the Aboriginal kids. You'll see the pride on the faces of non-Aboriginal kids as well, that they're learning this language'. Yuwaalaraay is now the school's compulsory language other than English under the New South Wales Board of Studies guidelines.

A kindergarten to Year 10 syllabus established in 2003 has sparked interest in mainstream Aboriginal language courses. Up to 5000 children across the state are now learning some of the oldest languages on Earth because they attend a mostly Indigenous school.

TAFE and the University of Sydney now offer new courses in Aboriginal languages, while a language centre at Nambucca Heads in northern New South Wales, is reviving the Gumbaynggir language for schools and elders. It allows them to learn the language denied them as children, and gives all Australians access to information about our country and its flora and fauna.

Not everyone agrees with bilingual education. Some people believe Australian schools should be English-only all the way through. By the 1990s, Northern Territory schools had switched back to the English-only model, but some schools call themselves 'Two-Way' and still use a bilingual model.

Australian children should not learn that James Cook 'discovered' Australia. After all, we knew we were already here! And the story is much more interesting and exciting than that. Cook was an incredible sailor, amongst the best of all time, but the Macassans, Portuguese and others came to Australia before him.

Today, Australia's schools, universities and technological colleges are developing courses that acknowledge us as Aboriginal and Torres Strait Islander students, just as Australia has embraced and respected the European and Asian cultures of immigrant Australians.

IMPROVING OUR CHILDREN'S EDUCATION

One of the biggest challenges for Australia's Indigenous children, and their teachers, is the widespread idea that they won't achieve anything. Government officials seem to care less about Indigenous students failing than they do about other students. It's easier to blame failure on the children or their communities.

It can be challenging to make changes, but the success of Dr Chris Sarra, former Principal of Cherbourg school in Queensland, proves that this is possible.

His rules for students (reinforced by staff and Principal) are:
- come to school every day
- work hard in the classroom
- be nice to the teacher
- be nice to other children
- work together
- be proud to be Aboriginal
- stand up for yourself.

His suggested tasks for teachers and principals as leaders are:
- supporting (best staff; teachers aides to broker relationships with parents)
- developing (teachers' professional development and leadership opportunities)
- monitoring (scrutinising what happens)
- challenging (asking the hard questions: would you accept this result for your own children?)
- intervening (doing the hard things).

Nearly every university around the country has an Indigenous studies centre that provides courses about Aboriginal or Indigenous life and culture. This centres also support Indigenous students by helping with accommodation and other issues in adjusting to life as a tertiary student.

KULBARDI PROVIDES 'WINGS TO FLY'

'Yorl koorliny Kulbardi Mia Mia. Nidja Noonookurt Nyinniny Kadadjinny Kowee Wallak' — Come here to the Kulbardi Aboriginal Centre. This is where you sit, learn, laugh and share.

It's obvious from the first words on the Kulbardi website at Murdoch University in Western Australia that you'll be introduced to Nyungar culture and language.

The Centre offers friendship and support and cultural strength to those who attend and encourages Indigenous students to stay and actively participate in tertiary studies.

The site's Kulbardi Kadjinini or 'Magpie Learning' cultural sector is available to all the university's students and aims to provide an 'overview of Nyungar cultures and life through the learning of the Nyungar language'.

Employment

Depending on where we live, we have worked in dual economies: in natural resources, via hunting and gathering, and in the waged economy. Although the effects of colonisation, through forced removals, dislocation, truncated education, racism, and so on have erected significant barriers to employment, our people have been the labour backbone of the pastoral and pearling industries, particularly in northern Australia. Each region has its own particular mix of disadvantages, so the community and elders have an important role to play in planning remedial action. Our median incomes are just 35 per cent of those of non-Indigenous Australians, so there is much to be learned from our successful communities.

Some communities have developed flourishing businesses, and the skills learnt in these enterprises have allowed people to begin other projects and take on further educational opportunities.

Successful enterprises

The Wathaurong community in Geelong has benefited from a partnership with the local council and government bodies. It offers property developers efficient services to deal with native title and heritage listings. This service provides employment, a climate of confidence for developers to proceed with their projects, and a positive relationship model for Indigenous and non-Indigenous people. The Wathaurong Co-op's factory produces glass art which is sold internationally, while we train as artists, glass craftspeople and business managers. The success of the operation is a source of much pride and a sense of independence in the community.

Local employment initiatives at Ceduna in South Australia cover a wide range of activities, including municipal maintenance, mechanical workshops, building enterprises, farming, aquaculture and horticultural projects. The Koonibba community also run employment training workshops to support these enterprises, and a recently opened fresh seafood and chicken retail outlet provides not only somewhere to sell their primary produce but also retail training for their young people.

Members of the Tweed Byron Local Aboriginal Land
Council and the NSW Fire Department working
together in northern New South Wales. Dhimurru
ranger monitoring turtles in Dhimurru Protected Area.

DHIMURRU INDIGENOUS PROTECTED AREA

Dhimurru is the Yolngu language word for the east wind
that brings rain. The Dhimurru Indigenous Protected Area is
located on Aboriginal land surrounding Nhulunbuy in north-
east Arnhem Land and covers about 92 000 hectares of land
and 9000 hectares of coastal waters. The Traditional Owners
of the area did not want a joint management arrangement and
the Dhimurru Land Management Aboriginal Corporation was
established in 1992. The corporation used many relationships
between two or more partners rather than the typical joint
management model. Both Aboriginal tradition and Western
science are used to care for the area, and this 'two-way'
approach is supported with strong infrastructure (from mining),
strong partnerships, reliable funding, strong decision-making
and the use of new idea, particularly in the marine areas, a
previously untried field.

We have a long history of fishing for abalone — Beryl Cruse and Liddy Stewart helped write a book, *Mutton Fish*, about it. At Bateman's Bay and Eden in New South Wales, communities now operate oyster leases and retail outlets for the produce.

With good education and support, enterprising communities from Redfern to Gosford, Lakes Entrance to Eden and Oenpelli to Broome

THE BOOM IN MINING

It has been estimated that $100 billion has been invested in mining in Western Australia since 2002. In 2008 there were 27 000 unemployed Indigenous people in Western Australia, despite the boom.

Professor Marcia Langton acknowledges the work being done by some mining companies to train and employ Indigenous people, but insists that more work is needed. In 2006 there was national employment parity with population, but she notes there are areas where the large majority of people are Indigenous, where the figures aren't as good. She believes the mining companies need support from the Commonwealth government.

Barry Taylor is Executive Chairman of Ngarda Civil and Mining Pty Ltd, the largest earth-moving company in Western Australia, which has its own training program. He believes the state government needs to do more. He acknowledges that the mining companies pay royalties and taxes, but, along with others, he believes that that revenue is spent 'down south', not in the areas where it is earned.

Some of the mining companies offer apprenticeships, training, mentoring and employment for Indigenous people, but the demand for labour still means that many staff fly in and fly out of remote areas. Barry Taylor would like to see more local employment, and investment in infrastructure and education.

Professor Langton has talked with mining employees and knows that despite the hard work and long shifts, people want good jobs and fair pay. Jobs in mining can offer this.

have set up businesses in the mining industry, catering and tourism, as employment consultants, and in the arts, media and the retail sectors.

Torres Strait Islander and Aboriginal men have worked on boats for subsistence and later for wages from the nineteenth century up until the 1960s.

Part of the exodus of Islanders to the mainland was in search of work when the pearling industry wound down, which began in the 1950s, and as a way to support families. Indigenous men worked cutting cane, but as this was only seasonal work they sought work further afield. Torres Strait Island men went as far as the Pilbara in Western Australia during the mining boom of the 1960s and 1970s. Some returned to their Islands; others remained and helped maintain their communities and culture, having obtained employment in other fields. Others found work on the railways, and some of the top teams were eventually wooed to national and overseas projects, with a Torres Strait Islander team holding a world speed record for track construction.

A Heritage of Leadership

Aboriginal society is characterised by its relatively egalitarian social life with high levels of autonomy for local groups who speak for distinct tracts of country. However, within groups, individual elders generally rise to prominence on the basis of their knowledge of the intricacies of ancestral creation and the relevance of this information to the performance of major ceremonies. The heritage of leadership by our elders is manifest today in the work of former and current politicians like Neville Bonner (our first Indigenous senator), Aden Ridgeway, Marion Scrymgour, and Linda Burney, jurists like Mick Dodson, Pat O'Shane, Michael Mansell, Larissa Behrendt and Rhonda Jacobsen, educators like Martin Nakata, John Lester, Marcia Langton, Mark Rose and Mary Ann Bin-Sallik, and human right activists such as Hannah McGlade. In South Australia, Yorta Yorta man Pastor Sir Douglas Ralph 'Doug' Nicholls was the Governor of South Australia from 1976 to 1977.

Vicki Matson-Green with her daughter, Tarni.

HIGH ACHIEVER

Vicki Maikutena Matson-Green has been included on the Tasmanian Honour Roll of Women for service to Aboriginal affairs.

'Aunty Vicki ... is one of the strongest Aboriginal advocates I know in this State', said Sharon Dennis in 2007.

Vicki Matson-Green is of the Palawa people and grew up in an extended family on Flinders Island. Her achievements are many. An advocate for the recognition of Aboriginal history and Aboriginal rights in Tasmania, she has undertaken higher education, been a champion for students, and an adviser to the University of Tasmania. She is active within the writing community, has published papers on the Palawa people and their history, and worked with an Aboriginal elder to help produce her biography. She's been a committee member within a range of organisations, including providing advice to arts bureaucrats. Her work with the Indigenous Services unit of Centrelink helped change the way that department related to Aboriginal people. Vicki is soon to move home to Flinders Island where she hopes to establish a garden centre with an arts café attached through which Tasmanian Aboriginal arts will be displayed and sold.

Our elders encourage our younger generations to pursue learning and civic involvement so as to forge a new way and a fair go that will allow all of us to contribute equally to the nation's future.

AUSTRALIA'S 'RENAISSANCE' MAN

His portrait features on Australia's $50 banknote, but few Australians know much about David Unaipon, who was a man of incredible achievements.

Born at the Point McLeay mission in South Australia (Raukkan) in 1872, Unaipon was the son of a Ngarrindjeri Aboriginal evangelist, James Ngunaitponi, and his wife, Nymbulda. An intelligent and visionary man denied a higher education, Unaipon had a love of science that was reflected in his ability for 'making things that worked'. He designed a sheep shearing handpiece which converted circular motion to lateral motion and lodged patents for various other inventions, including a helicopter based on the aerodynamics of the boomerang.

Desperate for his Aboriginal culture to be understood, Unaipon worked to ensure that 'an enduring record of our customs, beliefs and imaginings' were preserved — he believed there was a similarity between Christian and Aboriginal values. He represented Aboriginal people's views at two royal commissions (1913 and 1926) and inquiries into Aboriginal Affairs succeeded in influencing government policy.

Unaipon wrote stories and poetry. In 1930 his *Legendary Tales of the Australian Aborigines* was usurped and published under the name of William Ramsay Smith; it was not until 2001 that a new edition restored Unaipon's authorship. His role as a writer is honoured annually by the David Unaipon award.

In 2004 Frances Rings choreographed a dance piece for Bangarra Dance Theatre, influenced by Unaipon's obsession with perpetual motion, and his conception of a machine whose movement would be self-sustaining.

War Service

We have fought in every war in which Australia has been engaged and often with great distinction. Reg Saunders was the first Aboriginal commissioned officer and fought for his country in the Middle East, North Africa, Greece, Crete and New Guinea in World War II. Leonard Waters was Australia's only Aboriginal World War II fighter pilot. They are just two of the many distinguished servicemen and women.

Thousands of Aboriginal and Torres Strait Islanders served in Australian defence forces in World War I and World War II. Many more served in Vietnam and Korea, and then in the Somalia, Serbia, Timor, Iraq and Afghanistan.

Aboriginal serviceman Private Samuel Alexandra Peacock (Sam) Lovatt and his niece Alice Lovatt, an Aboriginal servicewoman, standing on a Melbourne street, 1942.

AT THE WAR'S FRONT

Torres Strait Islander women living on remote islands beyond the front line of Australia's north-eastern defences against Japanese aggression in 1942 were left in their communities to fend for themselves. All women and children living on the inner islands were evacuated south.

Two women remember:

When we were out fishing and the planes — twenty-five thirty — came over, we dig a hole and lie down in the sand and cover ourselves with our dress and put sand over us.

On Mabuiag Island the women witnessed fighting between Japanese and Allied planes overhead:

We could see them like white birds everywhere on top, and we can see the smoke when they fired the guns.

On Nagi the women, children and old people went a long way beyond the village, up the hill, and built houses with plaited mat walls and sheet iron or grass roofs, all camouflaged with branches and leaves. The old people found the disruption difficult. After one air alert a Nagi woman noted:

Our grandmother was a short little lady and she used to run in between us. She could not keep up. She said, 'Next time they come, leave me. Let that bomb fall on me.'

Even though legally excluded from serving in the armed forces, Aboriginal men fought at Gallipoli and the Western Front in World War I. Yet when they returned to Australia, almost all were denied rights given to other returned servicemen, including the soldier settlement scheme, which offered farming land to former soldiers. Not only were Victoria's Gunditjmara not offered settlements, but their reserve land was taken back and given to other soldiers.

A squad of the Torres Strait Light Infantry Battalion training in their company lines, Thursday Island, 1945.

'ONE AILAN MAN': TORRES STRAIT ISLANDER INFANTRY

From a population of a few thousand, nearly 1000 Torres Strait Islander recruits signed up to join Australia's war effort between 1942 to 1945. This was despite it being the pearling season, when many island men normally worked on the boats.

Fearful of the Japanese advance, the army allowed the Islanders to enlist. They later became the Torres Strait Light Infantry Battalion.

The Islanders had maintained their traditional island identities; now, in joining the Australian army, they fought side by side with other Australians. In wartime, they saw themselves working together as 'one ailan man'.

While the Torres Strait Islanders risked their lives defending Australia, they received only a third of the pay of other Australian soldiers. Frustrated at the discrimination and needing to take care of their families, in 1943 they decided to go on strike. The army agreed to raise the pay to two-thirds that of other army personnel. It wasn't until the 1980s that Indigenous soldiers received their back pay.

Making Decisions for our Communities

Reconciliation Australia is an organisation which recognises that the main ingredient in overturning disadvantage in our communities is making good decisions for those communities. Reconciliation Australia emphasises that good decision-making 'only comes about when Indigenous peoples have real power to make decisions about policies affecting their own communities'.

A crucial factor in the success of any program to improve our health, education and employment is to support and encourage our communities to manage our own services. To that end, Reconciliation Australia has arranged partnerships with BHP Billiton, the Australian National University and the governments of Western Australia and the Northern Territory to promote good governance skills and research.

Doctors, nurses and teachers have recommended for decades that the health and education services, particularly in remote communities,

Leroy Yarmirr being served by Sally Anne White at the Traditional Credit Union. Established in Milingimbi, in 1994, there are now twelve branches in the Northern Territory.

Central Queensland University masters graduate, Vanessa Seekee, left, being awarded the 2008 Queensland Premier's Reconciliation Award. She and husband, Liberty, won for their efforts to preserve Torres Strait Islander World War II history.

should be managed under the authority of those local communities. Local Land Councils and cooperatives have been delivering such services in some locations for decades. Care for pregnant women, after-school programs, kindergartens, elderly citizen homes, drug and alcohol rehabilitation, sports organisations, art and culture centres, housing cooperatives and archaeological services are just some of the success stories springing from community-controlled administration. Allowing our elders and communities to manage solutions, with access to sufficient staff and funds, is crucial for these programs to run successfully and efficiently.

The Aboriginal and Torres Strait Islander Commission (ATSIC) was established to provide us with some administrative control over our affairs at a regional and national level but in 2005 the Commonwealth government passed a law to disband it. While it is true that ATSIC had vocal critics in both the Indigenous and non-Indigenous communities, shutting it down and making the funds it administered available to

WUNAN SUCCESS

Wunan is an independent and not-for-profit organisation which supports long-term Aboriginal community development. The organisation's activities stretch over 236 246 square kilometres in the East Kimberley and reach about 15 000 people, of whom 40 per cent are Indigenous.

Wunan's purpose is to ensure that Aboriginal people in the East Kimberley enjoy the capabilities and opportunities necessary to make positive choices that lead to independent and fulfilling lives — essentially, to have dreams and a fair chance at achieving them.

Wunan's programs are based around four strategic areas: education and employment, accommodation and housing, community management support; and corporate governance and capacity.

- Wunan Business Assist acts as a 'skills bank'. It supports the growth and stability of organisations, providing services like bookkeeping, accounting, and governance support.
- Wunan Construction and Maintenance provides commercial building and maintenance services. It maintains a policy of employing and training young Aboriginal people.
- Wunan Pathways encourage the training and employment of Aboriginal people of all ages. Its programs include employment services and community partnerships aimed at encouraging a direct transition from school to work.
- Wunan Accommodation provides affordable accommodation and support for Aboriginal people working, studying or undertaking traineeships or apprenticeships.

mainstream government departments has undermined the operation of important community programs in health, education and culture (see p. 34, 39, 70).

Where our communities have been able to take an active and equal role in negotiating participation in mining, tourism, and heritage enterprises, the results have usually been advantageous for us.

Making legal decisions for our communities

The recognition of our customary law within the criminal justice system is a complex and difficult issue, which has been criticised and, in a few cases, sensationalised in the popular media; however, there are misconceptions about it in the wider Australian community. Customary law has been taken into account primarily in sentencing people convicted of crimes, not in judging their guilt or innocence.

The non-Indigenous criminal justice system sometimes emphasises punishment over rehabilitation in the way it deals with criminal behaviour. Our community-based approaches try to bridge the gap between the expectations of both sides, the victims and the accused.

One example is the use of the Circle Sentencing program, where community elders and a facilitator, along with the person convicted of the offence, and sometimes those who were the victims of the offence, meet in a circle. The matter is discussed and a joint decision is agreed about an appropriate sentence. Our elders provide no easy options, and some who work in the justice system believe that the sentences they hand out are tougher than those given in the society at large. However, the elders also work hard to keep young people out of the prison system.

Every state and territory now has an Aboriginal Legal Service.

In the Torres Strait, there has been some form of Islander local government since the 1890s and regional structures since 1939. Although the Queensland government maintained control until the 1980s, there has been an increase in Islander self-determination over time.

The Torres Strait Regional Authority is an Australian government statutory authority set up in 1994 to advise the Australian Minister for Indigenous Affairs on matters relating to the Torres Strait. It escaped the fate of the Aboriginal and Torres Strait Island Commission (ATSIC), which was dissolved in 2004. The officials who work for the authority think of, organise and run programs aimed at helping Torres Strait Islanders manage our own affairs in everything from economic development and employment to native title, housing and environmental health, based on our unique *Ailan Kastom bilong Torres Strait* — Torres Strait Islander culture.

ABORIGINAL LEGAL SERVICE

In June 1995, Rob Riley, CEO of the West Australian Aboriginal Legal Service, addressed the Secretary of the UN Committee on the Elimination of Racial Discrimination:

What we have been doing in trying to advance issues of Indigenous rights in this country has been in many respects quite profound. We have units that specialise in criminal law, civil law and family law. Since the Royal Commission, we have set up a land and heritage unit, a public interest unit and a community education and awareness unit. The public interest unit looks at human rights issues, test cases and law reform.

He went on to comment on the lack of state government funding:

[They've said] Nothing about community initiatives, nothing about dealing with issues that are causing these kids to get into the criminal justice system in the first place . . . It is important that we use our networks to distribute that information which enables indigenous people to bring about an accountability of Australian governments.

In 1995, *Telling Our Story* was published by the West Australian Aboriginal Legal Service. It examined the effect of government policies that removed thousands of Aboriginal children from their families.

Rob Riley, who was reunited with his family only after years spent in Sister Kate's Home, said, 'The report confirms a significant manifestation between removal from family and severe psychological, social and economic problems experienced by many Aboriginal people later in life'.

The Sea of Hands is ANTaR's primary public education
initiative and Australia's largest public art installation.
It has been installed in every major city and many
regional locations throughout Australia.

Resistance and Reconciliation

As a nation, Australia suffers because it has never confronted the fact that an entire continent was taken from its Indigenous peoples without treaties. Too few Australians are able to seriously examine our shared colonial past without averting their eyes from unpalatable facts. Some other countries have a better record of handling the tensions and differences of opportunity between their Indigenous and non-Indigenous people.

Since colonisation began in 1788, we have followed no single reactive strategy. Over time, depending on the circumstances and degree of governmental control, we have res sted, accommodated, worked towards reconciliation or combined these activities. Some among us call ourselves activists still, though our forms of activism have changed with the times.

Early Resistance

In the contact period of Aboriginal Australian history, we often opposed the European colonisers. Except by the Kalkadoon warrior at Battle Mountain in Queensland in 1884, it was guerilla warfare: resistance and attacks against a heavily armed invader. Early colonial newspapers were quick to label such hit and run tactics as 'treacherous' and colonial authorities declared martial law.

Nineteenth-century historians and commentators described large-scale frontier conflict, rather than an occasional skirmish. Henry Melville, in *The History of Van Diemen's Land*, commented that Aboriginal people were 'massacred without mercy . . . they were slaughtered in cold blood'. 'The historian,' he said, 'must ever lament, that he has to record outrages so inhuman and so unjust on the part of a British community. John West's 1852 *History of Tasmania*, while not critical of colonisation itself, provided extended and detailed accounts of white brutality. G. W. Rusden's *History of Australia* (1897) and Ernest Scott's popular *A Short History of Australia* (1916) noted the 'sheer brutality and treacherous murder by white settlers and their convict servants'.

Our various systems of organisation and control, established over thousands of years, were devised to best meet our needs. Traditionally, our governance was characterised by systems of land tenure that in some areas included descent group membership, relationship to country by birth in others, as well as complex systems of shared responsibility derived ultimately from the Dreaming. This regional division of responsibility was reflected in our response to colonial invasion after 1788, which was conducted at a strictly local level against individual transgressors. It was not until the early 1810s in Tasmania (1830s in New South Wales and 1840s in Victoria) that pan-Aboriginal resistance across local groups was organised.

Our forces were weakened by a combination of factors. In the late 1800s, we faced not only increasing numbers of British military forces but also their better guns and the raids of the Native Police, while we also suffered increased losses of life from disease and warfare, a situation not helped by our reduced access to shelter and food.

Often the settlers fought the war outside the law and were rarely brought before the courts to account for their actions. After the Myall Creek massacre in New South Wales in 1828, where at least twenty-eight Wirrayaraay people were killed by twelve armed stockmen, the perpetrators were tried before a court and seven convict shepherds were sentenced to death. Such was the outcry from the non-Indigenous public, that white men had been charged and found guilty, that the authorities were reluctant to allow such cases to be tried before courts again. Eighty years later views have changed and the area has been proclaimed as a National Heritage site.

At Coniston in the Northern Territory in 1929 at least thirty-one of us were killed in reprisal for the murder of Fred Brooks, a dingo trapper, although many believe the number of dead was closer to one hundred. Brooks was killed after his mistreatment of a Warlpiri woman but the police officer who led the raid was freed from blame. In every state and territory the authorities and courts went to elaborate lengths to protect perpetrators of violence against us.

NATIVE POLICE

Aboriginal police and police trackers played important roles during the nineteenth and twentieth centuries in colonial Australia. Seen by some today as traitors, our people's involvement with policing was an adaptation to changing circumstances on the frontier.

The native police forces were all male, but both men and women worked as trackers, and used their bush expertise when the need arose. They were usually given a token payment, plus rations for their families.

The first 'native police' began work in 1837 in Victoria. Paramilitary in nature, they were provided with uniforms and horses and cooperated with the colonisers, deterring attacks on pastoral properties. They also captured non-Indigenous offenders and later provided service on the gold diggings and the transport of gold back to Melbourne.

The native police were selective about whom they chose to track, pursuing people from other Aboriginal groups but claiming not to be able to follow the tracks of their own people.

The New South Wales and Queensland native police had a reputation for violence. They were ordered to 'disperse' any large groups of Aboriginal people, which was understood and acknowledged by senior police as shooting them, and preventing them from meeting and engaging in ceremonies.

In the Northern Territory, some Aboriginal people who were imprisoned were offered shorter sentences in return for their agreeing to work. Aboriginal people were forbidden to have guns, but some took up weapons and carried out attacks against their enemies. On occasions, they were blamed for attacks on Aboriginal people by non-Indigenous police.

The methods of dispossession used in Australia were both spontaneous responses and a calculated campaign. Many of the men involved in implementing them had undertaken similar acts of dispossession in India, Africa and America. As part of the process of dispossession, it was useful to portray our people as a lesser branch of the human family, who neither 'tilled the soil' nor 'worked'. They came to be regarded by the colonists as people living off the land rather than producers. A self-serving myth emerged to which parliaments, courts and media still sometimes contribute.

Introduced diseases like smallpox, syphilis and influenza that came to Australia with the colonists (though smallpox may have been introduced in the north by the Macassans), took a significant toll on our populations. However, some theorists who consider disease to be the major a cause of our population decline may be discounting the extent to which violence on the frontier had an impact on our numbers.

In the Torres Strait in the 1860s, European vessel masters sought trepang and trochus shell. Their crews included South Sea Islanders and later, Filipinos and Japanese. Vast quantities of pearl shell were discovered in the 1870s and more ships arrived. Armed with guns, some the crew members were able to overwhelm the Islanders. Some Islanders were safer than others, but women were abducted, gardens raided and men co-opted for work. In 1871 the London Missionary Society landed two missionary teachers on Erub (Darnley) Island and soon all the islands had been visited by missionaries. By the end of the decade, communities without missionary teachers were asking for them. The Islanders believed that the missionaries could protect them from the violent acts of foreign seamen. The new religion was quickly accepted and absorbed. For nearly forty years the London Missionary Society maintained strong control in the Straits, filling both a spiritual and political vacuum.

The Queensland government's Acts of Annexation of some islands in 1872, and then in 1879 of the remainder, were prompted more by fear of rival colonial powers and a desire to control the increasingly lucrative

COLONIAL GRAZIERS AND LAND

In most cases, police took over where the official and unofficial armies left off. As late as the 1960s in Queensland, the government used police to force people away from the waterholes and grain-harvesting areas of their traditional country, land the colonisers demanded for sheep and cattle. Colonial graziers failed to understand the nature and strength of Indigenous attachment to land; they simply wanted the land for their stock and thought that one area of land was the same as another to us, so some of them shot, legislated and convicted until they got it. Sir Thomas Mitchell in 1846 mused on the inevitability of dispossession even as he rode through miles of grain harvested by Aboriginal people on the banks of the Narran River in Queensland. 'I could not help but reflect that the white man's cattle would soon trample these holes into a quagmire of mud, and destroy the surrounding verdure and pleasant freshness forever.' Just as Mitchell predicted, many of the graziers resorted to violence when faced with resistance for possession of such productive land.

marine industry than to protect the Islanders. The role of Government Resident was created, and the Honourable John Douglas was appointed to be responsible for the Islanders, among other duties. He remained in this job for eighteen years, a period marked by his easygoing brand of paternalism. When he died in 1904, the Chief Protector placed the Islanders under the same controls as other Aboriginal people. Queensland's native affairs policy was still emerging, but it was later to become a model for the rest of Australia. Two of its elements were extended instruction, while keeping us socially isolated from European society, and producing obedient unskilled workers. The *Torres Strait Islander Act 1939* followed, with further legislation in 1965, 1971–79, 1984 and 1985.

Protection Acts

Protection Acts were passed in every state following Victoria's Aboriginal Protection Act in 1869. Amendments over the following years made them increasingly restrictive. They operated until the second half of the twentieth century, controlling the lives of Aboriginal and Torres Strait Island people. By 1881, New South Wales had an Aboriginal Protector and later a Board for the Protection of Aborigines. A new law in 1915 gave the Board the right to assume control and custody of Aboriginal children and to remove them to 'such care and control as it thinks best'. In 1940, the New South Wales Board was reorganised into the Aborigines Welfare Board, which controlled Aboriginal lives in New South Wales until 1969. The Board had a high degree of control and the ability to force us to do things, but offered us much less welfare and protection than we had under earlier arrangements.

Missions, Reserves and Stations

The dispossession of Aboriginal and Torres Strait Islander people caused problems of economic and social disruption and pangs of conscience for colonial Australia.

Aboriginal people were desperately trying to scratch out a living, as we were moved off our country and had little access to our usual bush foods. We had to rely instead on rations distributed by missions, managers of government reserves and pastoralists. We were often accused by colonists of stealing basic items like flour, sheep and clothes. Some colonists were concerned simply for the loss of their possessions; others were disturbed by our obvious distress. In the Torres Strait we were subjected to controls over our movement.

Colonial governments reacted in different ways. Most created reserves (areas of land) onto which we were moved, often taking us away from our country, our sources of food, our sacred sites and our families. Many of us adapted to these changes and engaged in agricultural pursuits such as growing hops and establishing craft industries. We had some freedom of movement in the early days and were able to work but the

REGRET AND DISGUST

My heart is filled with regret and disgust. First because you were taken down by those who were supposed to be your help and guide through life. What a wicked conception, what a fallacy. Under the so-called pretence and administration of the Board, governmental control etc. I say deliberately. The whole damnable thing has got to stop and by God[s] help it shall, make no mistake. No doubt, they are trying to exterminate the Noble and Ancient Race of sunny Australia. Away with the damnable insulting methods. Give us a hand, stand by your own Native Aboriginal Officers and fight for liberty and freedom for yourself and your children.

Thus Fred Maynard, Aboriginal activist, wrote to a young Aboriginal girl in 1927; one who had been abused within the government-operated Aboriginal apprenticeship system.

Aurukun Presbyterian mission, far north Queensland, 1962.

LIFE ON THE FRONTIER

In *Very Big Journey*, Melissa Lucashenko tells us:

Hilda Muir was born at Manangoora, near the small outback town of Borroloola in about 1920. It was an era of pearl luggers and bullock drays, and, as a child, Hilda heard graphic first-hand accounts about the dangers of wild white men and their guns. For the Yanyuwa people, the sound of shooting still resonated through their homelands, which were only then coming under the firm control of white authorities. Hilda was born, in other words, on the very frontier of modern Australia.

Hilda herself remembers being taken away from her family:

When that good old horse took me away from Borroloola on the long journey to Darwin, it changed my life forever . . . I stopped being an Aboriginal girl and became a half-caste girl. From someone who'd had so much, I was now someone who had nothing, with no past and an unknown future.

laws were changed over time, restricting our abilities to travel and to lead lives over which we had some control. All the laws were designed to strengthen control of the different state governments over us. All the Acts enabled the removal of children, especially those of mixed descent. For example, the New South Wales Act allowed the forceful removal of children in order to 'resocialise them'.

Chief Protectors were usually senior bureaucrats who, in turn, appointed other local protectors, usually missionaries and police. Their powers were wide-ranging. Outwardly, this was to protect us from the influence of non-Indigenous Australians. At the same time, missionaries from the various denominations offered to take over our care, and convert us to Christianity. State governments were keen to adopt such relatively cheap measures of control.

In the Torres Strait two levels of discrimination shaped society, some of it similar to what was happening in Aboriginal Australia. Europeans held positions of power in industry, commerce, government, religion and the military. Non-Europeans were subordinated but divided into two further groups: Indigenous Islanders and foreigners. Special laws prevented Japanese divers from moving up in society. The government sought to define and contain people. While other divers dealt directly with their employers, Islanders had to deal through a government which controlled their earnings and their employment.

Cinemas, schools and churches were segregated and we were excluded from hotels, and from Thursday Island at night. We were not able to travel freely and were made to live apart, while being offered fewer health and educational opportunities than non-Indigenous people.

The influence of the Church

The Christian Church was closely integrated with our daily life and provided a hierarchical rank for men. In the 1890s, the responsibility for law and order, previously given to *mamooses* (someone acting as a chief and given power by the authorities) by a Queensland magistrate on the advice of a missionary, Samuel McFarlane, passed to the government teacher.

Bishop Kawemi Dai was the first Anglican Torres Strait Islander bishop. He was consecrated in 1986 on Thursday Island in a service which combined Anglican and traditional elements. In 2002 Meriam Bishop Saibo Mabo was consecrated national bishop to the Torres Strait Islander people.

On the mainland, the success of the missions varied according to the financial support they received and the personalities of their directors. Some, like Corranderk in Victoria, were happy, productive and economically stable villages until government policy changed and the station was disbanded. Some clergymen were enlightened and treated us well, but all were united in their view that until we became Christians we had no hope of civilisation.

AUSTRALIA'S FIRST ABORIGINAL ANGLICAN BISHOP

Arthur Malcolm was in tears as the cavalcade of late-model cars moved towards Yarrabah Aboriginal community. Two columns of painted dancers snaked forward singing a Gunganjdji welcome. The road was lined with Yarrabah people and visitors. Traditionally dressed Torres Strait Islanders joined Aboriginal dancers who clapped boomerangs and brandished spears. An Aboriginal elder presented Arthur Malcolm with a woomera — a symbol of his authority among them and of his spiritual power. Priests, deacons and Indigenous bishops from other countries joined the overflowing crowd who clapped and cheered Arthur Malcolm. He was their new bishop, the first Aboriginal bishop in the Anglican Church. It was 13 October 1985.

Bishop Malcolm's father was Kokobera from south of Kowanyama in the western Cape York Peninsula and his mother Olkolo from the Alice River north of Kowanyama, sent to Yarrabah under the Queensland system of removals. But Bishop Malcolm was born and raised at Yarrabah. His first job, a common one for young Yarrabah men, was on the sanitary cart. As a young man he left to train as an evangelist in the Anglican Church Army.

'You know, we had Jesus before you whitefellows came,' Catholic Deacon Monty Prior once said. Nowadays, Yarrabah, one of the old mission communities, has become a centre of Christian revival, expressing an Aboriginal understanding and spirituality.

Reserves

Aware of the effects of violence, diseases and removal from their land, the colonial government, believed that Aboriginal people were doomed to extinction. Aboriginal Protection Acts were established so that Indigenous Australians could be looked after during their remaining years.

Meriam Bishop Saibo Mabo.

The effect of these laws left those on the reserves as wards of the state, with members of the Protection Boards as their legal guardians. While protection may have been the main aim of the Acts, in practice the Boards were given complete power and control over the lives of the Aboriginal people under their care.

Some reserves operated as prisons. Much has been written about Moore River in Western Australia, for example. Children were separated from their families and lived in dormitories. Those thought to be acting badly were placed in 'The Boob', a prison within a prison. Escape was difficult. The grandmother of Aboriginal activist Rob Riley spent almost twenty-five years in Moore River, because permission to leave required that she leave her children behind.

Depending on the place and the people in charge, the treatment was in some cases physically cruel and authoritarian. Those in charge were often contemptuous of us. For example, in some cases women had to apply in writing to the mission superintendent if they needed underwear. The mission would then choose and make the purchase out of the women's own money. The Western Australian protection system, under AO Neville, was particularly destructive in its interference in even the most ordinary and private aspects of our lives.

Stories from Palm Island in north Queensland have shocked many with their examples of violence and brutality, especially by police. A physically beautiful place, Palm Island was originally established as a prison. People who didn't share the same language and culture were sent there for minor offences: famous athlete Cathy Freeman's grandfather was sent there because he refused to sign an employment agreement, something he wasn't required to do. Cathy Freeman's mother, a generation later, requested permission to leave Palm Island to spend Christmas with her family in Cherbourg. She was refused.

THE PILBARA STRIKE

One of the earliest cases of our resistance to the control of labour was when Don McLeod, a non-Indigenous unionist, and Dooley Bin Bin and Clancy McKenna, stockmen, led what's known as the Pilbara Strike in Western Australia in 1946. Eight hundred stockmen representing twenty-three Aboriginal groups struck in protest at the poor conditions and the failure of pastoralists to pay wages.

The strike paralysed twenty sheep stations and the pastoralists tried to break the strike by withholding rations. None of the stockmen returned to the stations, preferring to live off the land or go mining for themselves. The strikers remained firm despite thirty-two of them being arrested at Warrawagine Station and being chained by the neck for ten days.

Dooley Bin Bin and McKenna were jailed for three months but the strike continued until the state government negotiated with McLeod and promised reformed conditions of employment. As soon as the strike was called off, the reforms were scrapped. (See also p. 105)

Station life

Many people across northern Australia maintained contact with their country by living on pastoral leases, government reserves and Christian missions. In doing so, we provided an accessible workforce for pastoralists. The men who lived on the stations worked as seasonal drovers and labourers, while the women were employed throughout the year as domestics, with some women also working with stock on horseback. The women were at risk of sexual abuse from non-Indigenous stockworkers.

Women worked in the buffalo hide industry in the Northern Territory (c.1936). After defleshing the hides, they washed, drained, salted and stacked them. Five days later they were hung on racks, then folded for carrying to river landings.

Pastoralists were responsible for the distribution of government-issued rations to those of us who were too old to work. However, in reality they dispensed rations as they chose, sometimes withholding them as a method of discipline. This had a devastating effect on the health of those with limited access to bush tucker. Pastoralists justified not paying Aboriginal workers a cash wage on the basis of poor returns and our supposed unreliability. However, the economy of pastoral Australia was sustained by our cheap labour.

In our demands for a fair wage we refused to undertake some tasks, and on occasions, we went on strike. Our initial demands for a fair wage and better treatment of our women later translated into a demand for land (see p. 109–11).

With help from the North Australia Workers Union, the Northern Territory Cattle Station Industry Award Case was held and in 1966 a decision was made that granted equal wages to Aboriginal people.

Although long overdue, the Equal Wages Award, and the poor planning of its implementation in 1968, had devastating consequences. Pastoralists refused to employ us and we were exiled from our land. In the subsequent exodus into towns, we faced the dangers of access to

CORRANDERK FARMING SUCCESS

The mission at Corranderk near Healesville in Victoria is a good example of farming success. The Corranderk farm won awards at the Melbourne Show for its hops and other produce, but neighbouring farmers resented the success and combined with the detractors of Indigenous progress to erode government support for the mission. The Corranderk mission people got on well with the manager, John Green, who allowed some self-determination and had genuine respect for the people under his control, but the mission was always under threat from those contemptuous of us. The debate raged without resolution for another two years but greedy men and unsympathetic politicians finally drove the Corranderk people from their home.

alcohol, the loss of our skills and our self-esteem. Many communities are still recovering from these losses.

Missionaries and other humanitarians who actively supported our right to justice and a fair go were sometimes removed, often following strident media campaigns against them. For example, the Reverend Gribble was severely criticised in the nineteenth century by the West Australian press, pastoralists and politicians when he tried to intervene on behalf of Aboriginal people cruelly treated by non-Indigenous colonists.

Other well-meaning clergymen and colonial settlers, anxious to uphold decent civil values in our treatment, were ridiculed, silenced or censured and in time most missions were broken up so that surrounding pastoralists could have access to their land. The Buntingdale mission, established at Birregurra in Victoria in 1839, had been harassed for years by pastoralists accusing it of incompetence and the wastage of public money. Several of those leading the complaint, like the grazier William Roadknight, acquired the land when the mission was eventually abandoned in response to public criticism of Aboriginal protectorates and missions.

Aboriginal community outside the church at Lake Tyers with Reverend John Bulmer, c. 1910.

CAPE BARREN ISLAND

Cape Barren Island is one of several islands in the Furneaux group, off the north-east coast of Tasmania, in Bass Strait. Some descendants of Aboriginal women and sealers moved from Flinders Island to Cape Barren Island, where a reserve was formally established in 1881. Over time, the Cape Barren Islanders were forced to let the Tasmanian government take control of their lives. Rather than helping them, the government demanded they move to the mainland, or their children would be taken away from them. By the 1950s, child welfare laws were used increasingly to remove children, with some parents being imprisoned for neglect. The removed children were fostered to non-Indigenous couples or sent to homes. In 1973 the government established the Aboriginal Information Service, which helped to reduce the number of removals of children. The Aboriginal Information Service is now called the Tasmanian Aboriginal Legal Service. In 1984 the Tasmanian government decided it would place children with Indigenous families.

Tasmanian Aboriginal elder, Ida West, has many memories of growing up on Cape Barren Island, especially cooking:

> We used to make a brown stew in the old iron pots. There is grilled mutton-birds, fried mutton-birds, baked mutton-birds with onions and stuffing, curried mutton-birds with rice, sea pie and salted birds. For smoked mutton-birds we used to thread the birds on a stick and put them over a drum and keep the fire in the drum for four to six weeks.
>
> We made kangaroo tail soup and brawn. We would dip the kangaroo tails in hot water and scrape the skin off.
>
> We had coupons to buy meat, sugar, tea, butter and clothes. We made our own soap out of dripping and we used mutton-bird oil for rubbing our chests for flu. Garlic in your shoes was a remedy for whooping cough. We would boil the buzzies from the vine of the bush and bottle. We ate grass tree bread which is the meat of the tree — white in colour and sweet in taste. We loved it.
>
> All my people cooked fruit cakes with mutton-bird fat dripping. The women were good cooks.

Some pastoralists with designs on the land, maligned the Protectors as lazy and ineffectual do-gooders. In time most Protectorate lands were taken over by governments for use by pastoralists and farmers. Land from some mission stations was offered to returned soldiers, called 'soldier settlers', after World War I and II.

Under the various Land Rights Acts, beginning with the South Australian *Aboriginal Land Trust Act 1966* (SA) and the better known *Aboriginal Land Rights (Northern Territory) Act 1976* (Cth), many of us who remained on the 'Mish', as government reserves and missions were called in some parts of the country, were granted ownership of our land. In Victoria, mission stations such as Lake Tyers and Lake Condah are now under our control; similarly at Point McLeay in South Australia and other former reserves in New South Wales, but not Western Australia where the land was not transferred.

Activism and Representation

Fred Maynard founded the Australian Aboriginal Progressive Association (AAPA) in 1924 in New South Wales. It organised street rallies, held well-publicised regional and metropolitan meetings and showed great skill

HOW MUCH HAS CHANGED?

The position of the remnant of the original owners of this land . . . is a blot on State and Church alike. The fact that certain aborigines are camped under petrol tins and without certain knowledge of where their next meal is coming from is a reflection of our boastful civilization. We may claim that we are not responsible for the actions of the original British invaders who violated their homes, shot, poisoned, burned and mutilated the natives; but we cannot claim immunity from the conditions existing at the present time, and what should not be tolerated for one moment longer than it will take to rectify matters.

Elizabeth McKenzie Hatton, non-Indigenous activist, *Daylight* on 30 October 1926.

in using newspaper coverage, letter-writing campaigns and petitions. It collaborated with the international black movement through Maynard's connections with Marcus Garvey, first president of the Universal Negro Improvement Association in the USA. Sadly, the Australian Aboriginal Progressive Association's demands still strike a chord today: Aboriginal rights to land, stopping Aboriginal children being taken from their families, and defending a distinct Aboriginal cultural identity.

The humble petition of the free Aborigines Inhabitants of V[an] D[ieman's] L[and] now living upon Flinders Island, in Bass's Straits &c & &c.

Most humbly showeth,

That we Your Majesty's Petitioners are your free Children that we were not taken Prisoners but freely gave up our Country to Colonel Arthur then the Governor after defending ourselves.

Your Petitioners humbly state to Y[our] M[ajesty] that Mr Robinson made for us & with Col. Arthur an agreement which we have not lost from our minds since & we have made our part of it good.

Your Petitioners humbly tell Y[our] M[ajesty] that when we left our own place we were plenty of People, we are now but a little one.

Your Petitioners state they are a long time at Flinders Island & had plenty of Superintendents & were always a quiet and free People & not put into Gaol.

Your Majesty's petitioners pray that you will not allow Dr. Jeanneret to come again among us as our Superintendent as we hear he is to be sent another time for when Dr Jeanneret was with us many Moons he used to carry Pistols in is pockets & threaten'd very often to shoot us & make us run away in fright...

Excerpt of Petition to Her Majesty Queen Victoria, 17 February 1846, signed by Walter George Arthur, Chief of the Ben Lomond Tribes, King Alexander, John Allen, Augustus, Davey Bruny, King Tippoo, Neptune, Washington, which called on British moral values rather than making a proclamation of rebellion.

Strikes and Protests

In January 1936, the Torres Strait Islanders working on the company boats fishing in the Strait went on strike, protesting against the constraints they experienced under the Aboriginal Protection Act. Non-violent and organised secretly, using Islander networks to transmit messages, the strike led to the *Torres Strait Islanders Act 1939*. This resulted in Torres Strait Islanders being distinguished in law from Aboriginal people legislatively, although the government still retained enormous control over their lives. The Queensland government allowed the creation of an inter-island organisation, known since 1984 as the Island Co-ordinating Council.

On 26 January 1938, we observed the first 'Day of Mourning'. While other Australians took part in the official celebrations of the 150th anniversary of the first fleet of British settlers landing at Botany Bay

A blackboard proclaims 'Day of Mourning' at an Aboriginal-only event. By 5pm a resolution of indignation and protest had been moved.

in New South Wales, we took part in a protest. William Cooper, the founder of the Australian Aborigines League, was deeply disappointed at the lack of progress in his attempts to encourage the Commonwealth government to make reforms in Aboriginal administration. He persuaded John Patten and William Ferguson, leaders of the Aborigines Progressive Association (APA), to organise a protest. About 100 Aboriginal people, and a few non-Aboriginal people, attended a conference on the day. A later deputation presented the Prime Minister with a proposed national policy for Aboriginal people but this was rejected on the pretext that the Commonwealth had limited constitutional responsibility for Aboriginal affairs. Patten wrote the manifesto, 'Aborigines Claim Citizenship Rights!' and we now remember 26 January as 'Invasion Day' or 'Survival Day'.

Assimilation

In 1939, John McEwen, the Commonwealth Minister for the Interior, announced a 'New Deal', but this was not in response to the manifesto of the Aborigines Progressive Association or demands from other Aboriginal organisations. This was the first announcement of assimilation as a Commonwealth government policy. Overall, the idea of assimilation was a shift from the idea of biological absorption — where children of mixed descent were taken away and raised as white, and it was thought that the rest of us would die out — to an idea of social and cultural assimilation. The Commonwealth government wanted

> [the] raising of their status so as to entitle them by right and by qualification to the ordinary rights of citizenship, and to enable them and help them to share with us the opportunities that are available in their own native land.

In New South Wales, assimilation had been introduced in 1940 when the Aborigines Welfare Board replaced the old Aborigines Protection Board. It was not until after World War II that the other states began to respond to humanitarian demands for a policy change. For example, the Commonwealth paid child endowment and the old age pensions to those of us who met the eligibility criteria.

In 1951, Paul Hasluck was appointed as Commonwealth Minister for Territories. He introduced a new policy of assimilation, which was adopted by the states, although Victoria and Tasmania claimed to have no real 'Aboriginal problem'. The policy of assimilation stated that:

[All] Aborigines shall attain the same manner of living as other Australians, enjoying the same rights and privileges, accepting the same responsibilities, observing the same customs and being influenced by the same beliefs, hopes and loyalties of other Australians.

By the mid-1960s, opposition to assimilation was strengthening and new policies, aimed more at integration, were being introduced. The Whitlam government cast aside assimilation as Commonwealth government policy in December 1972. Instead, a new policy, self-determination, was introduced. This completed the shift in policy development from protection to assimilation to self-determination.

Citizenship

After the 1940s the various state governments gave citizenship rights to some of us on condition that we gave up our traditional lives and stayed away from other Aboriginal people. People who received citizenship papers were no longer considered to be Aboriginal.

The 1967 Referendum

The year 1967 saw the culmination of a valiant campaign fought by Federal Council for the Advancement of Aboriginals and Torres Strait Islanders (FCAATSI) and others to encourage the Australian people to accept a referendum to change the Constitution. The change would allow Aboriginal people to be included in the census, and to enable the Commonwealth to make laws for Aboriginal and Torres Strait Islander people. In the drafting of the Australian Constitution, the colonies had said they wanted to retain their powers to make laws concerning the Aboriginal people within their territory, including those laws that discriminated against them. The Constitution therefore specifically prohibited the federal government from making laws in relation to

ALBERT NAMATJIRA AND CITIZENSHIP

Albert Namatjira is one of Australia's best-known artists, whose landscape paintings made him famous in Australia and overseas.

Namatjira was baptised when his parents adopted Christianity. He lived a mission life in his early years, but was later taught traditional Aranda laws and customs by his elders.

Namatjira's introduction to painting came when he volunteered to show painter Rex Batterbee good places to paint. In exchange, Rex taught Albert how to paint in watercolours. He was a gifted and swift learner whose landscapes, closer to a Western style than one of the more traditional Indigenous artforms, quickly became popular.

Although famous, Namatjira was subject to the discriminatory laws faced by his people and his plans to lease a cattle station and build a house in Alice Springs were blocked. Public outrage pushed the government to grant both he and his wife full citizenship in 1957.

Unfortunately, the inconsistency in the treatment of Aboriginal people caught up with Namatjira. In 1958, he was charged by the police with supplying alcohol to Aboriginal people. As a citizen he was allowed to drink, but he wasn't allowed to share alcohol with his friends and family. After being jailed for two months, he was released in poor health and died a year later.

Besides the legacy of his painting, Namatjira contributed much to the cause of Aboriginal people. Members of his family now carry on the tradition of painting.

Aboriginal people. It was hoped that the referendum would allow the federal government to overturn such laws and better protect Aboriginal and Torres Strait Islander people.

With its 90.77 per cent 'Yes' vote, the referendum was passed in all six states. It remains one of the most successful national campaigns in our history.

Handover of the Gurindji Cattle Station mining lease,
Wave Hill, August 1973.

WAVE HILL WALK-OFF

The Gurindji people (Aboriginal stockmen and their families)
took part in one of the most protracted industrial disputes
in Australian history. They walked off Wave Hill station, 700
kilometres south of Darwin in the Northern Territory, in 1966,
and captured national media attention. The land was leased by
Lord Vestey of London but the Gurindji, in seeking better pay
and conditions — with the support of unions and many private
citizens, writers and politicians — defied the laws that treated
them unfairly. Their cause was taken up around the country
and it grew into a fight for land rights, which resulted in the
Aboriginal Land Rights (Northern Territory) Act in 1976. Every
state except Tasmania and Western Australia then passed some
form of land rights legislation. Vincent Lingiari and his people
had focused public attention on Indigenous working conditions
and the restrictions that the vast private landholdings placed
upon the lives of Aboriginal people. The walk-off and strike
were landmark events in the struggle for Aboriginal land rights
and a large celebration, Freedom Day, is held at Kalkaringi
(Wave Hill) to remember the event.

Limited positive changes have been made to the lives of Aboriginal and Torres Strait Islander people since the 1967 referendum, and a close examination of the campaign and the changes to the Constitution reveal that there were limits to what might be expected.

Right to vote

The Australian Constitution said that 'in reckoning the numbers of people of the Commonwealth, or of a State or other part of the Commonwealth, aboriginal natives shall not be counted' (Section 127 xxvi). A few of us could vote before Federation in 1901 and kept the right after it. The Commonwealth *Electoral Act 1962* gave us the right to register and vote but voting was not compulsory. Full voting rights were not granted federally until Aboriginal and Torres Strait Islander people were required to register on the electoral roll in 1984.

New protests and the move towards land rights

In 1965, Charles Perkins, one of our first university graduates, led a group of our people and supporters on a 'Freedom Ride', a bus tour of outback New South Wales. The action was based on the US Freedom Rides, and sought to highlight blatant racism. At that time, we were barred from using public swimming pools in many Australian country communities. The Freedom Riders caused an enormous controversy across the nation as Australians were shown the true nature of race relations.

In 1963 the Yolngu people of Yirrkala in north-east Arnhem Land presented a bark petition to the Commonwealth Parliament. It was their response to the threat to their country posed by bauxite mining. These documents are the first traditional documents recognised by the Commonwealth Parliament. They combined traditional bark painting with text typed on paper. The painted designs proclaim Yolngu Law, revealing the people's traditional relationship to the land. The text is in English and Gumatj languages. Although the Yolngu didn't achieve the constitutional change they wanted, they helped pave the way for the recognition of Indigenous rights in Australian law. The following

Galarrwuny Yunupingu (far left) at the presentation of the Yirrkala petition on land rights to then Aboriginal Affairs Minister Ian Viner (far right) 1977. The petition had been handed to the Australian parliament in 1963.

court case, known as the *Gove Land Rights Case* in 1971, ended with the court rejecting the Rirratjingu clan's claim because their relationship to the land didn't fit the European concept of 'property', despite the court acknowledging that we had a 'subtle and elaborate system' of 'social rules and customs' that 'provided a stable order of society'. The judge was bound by early decisions that had said that regardless of the facts, as a matter of British law, Aboriginal people had no recognisable system of law.

The Tent Embassy

Other attempts were made through the courts for the return of stolen land but in each case they were thwarted by legal argument or political intervention. Tired of having legitimate claims denied, on Australia Day 1972, a number of Indigenous activists erected a tent on the lawns of Old Parliament House in Canberra. The protesters told the police they would

The Tent Embassy in front of Old Parliament House, 2002.

stay until the government granted land rights. The Embassy's petition, a five-point plan, addressed Aboriginal ownership of existing reserves and settlements (including rights to mineral deposits), ownership of land in the capital cities (including mineral rights), preservation of all sacred sites in all parts of the continent, six million dollars in compensation, and full rights of statehood for the Northern Territory.

Despite various attempts to dismantle it using police force, local ordinances, planning guidelines and direct negotiation (even attempts to burn it down), the Embassy remains on the lawns of Old Parliament House. It has been the centre of protest and the starting point for marches on Parliament demanding sovereignty and a treaty. Authorities have found it difficult to counter the Tent Embassy's mixture of persistent grass-roots politics and symbolism, with some Aboriginal people now talking about the site's sacredness. Called an embassy because it represents a displaced nation, in 1995 it was listed on the Australian Heritage Commission's National Estate.

The Aboriginal Tent Embassy, like Perkins' Freedom Ride, became a powerful symbol of resistance and cultural revival. It remains as a thorn in the side of the Australian conscience, reminding Australians that the work of forging a treaty has hardly begun.

Deaths in custody

In 1987 a Royal Commission investigated the social, cultural and legal issues involved in the deaths of Indigenous Australians while in police custody and prison. The 1991 *Royal Commission into Aboriginal Deaths in Custody* report provides harrowing reading. At that time, Aboriginal people made up 14 per cent of the total prison population and were up to fifteen times more likely to be in prison than non-Aboriginal Australians. In the decade following the report, deaths in police custody declined but deaths in prisons rose dramatically. Aboriginal deaths in custodial environments are still alarmingly high. To this date, few of the report's recommendations have been carried out.

The modest proposals of the report are designed to interrupt and reverse this insidious cycle. Strategies like mandatory sentencing will always disproportionately affect Aboriginal Australians, who are already over-represented in the criminal justice system.

Working through organisations

Another strand in the movements towards land rights was the establishment of the first national organisation for Indigenous people, the Federal Council for the Advancement of Aborigines. It was later known as FCAATSI, the Federal Council for the Advancement of Aboriginals and Torres Strait Islanders. FCAATSI, which included supportive non-Indigenous people in its early years, took a leading role in the success of the 1967 referendum. After the referendum win, FCAATSI became an all-Indigenous body (see p. 107).

In 1987, the federal government established the Aboriginal and Torres Strait Islander Commission or ATSIC (see p. 82). The new Commission combined some existing government organisations and took on the functions of the federal departments of Aboriginal Affairs, the Aboriginal Development Commission and Aboriginal Hostels.

Aboriginal Hostels Limited across Australia provides
temporary accommodation and community support to
Aboriginal and Torres Strait Islander peoples.

Attempts by earlier governments to involve us included the National
Aboriginal Conference and, before that, the National Aboriginal
Consultative Committee, which the government of the time found to be
assertive and confrontational. ATSIC later took over the representative
functions of the National Aboriginal Conference.

All three organisations were created by governments with little
input from our communities. The organisations were constrained
by government legislation, parts of which were created for political
purposes rather than to achieve things for our people. ATSIC was
meant to represent different regions through elections, but it was also
responsible for delivering programs. Funding was generally inadequate
for the organisation's needs. The ATSIC commissioners found themselves
unsure of their roles. Staff reported to the ATSC Board but also the
Minister. The disbanding of ATSIC in March 2004 was done without
proper consultation with Aboriginal leaders, and the government went
ahead despite the findings of its own review of ATSIC. Even if flawed,

The Northern Land Council uses the rainbow serpent as part of its identity because of its importance in creation stories across Australia. The rainbow serpent story is closely linked to land, water, life, social relationships and fertility.

CARING FOR COUNTRY

The Northern Land Council, one of several Aboriginal Land Councils around the country, began work in 1973. Its role is to represent traditional Aboriginal landowners and Aboriginal people in the Top End of the Northern Territory.

Consulting with traditional landowners and other Aboriginal people with an interest in land is one of the Council's most important responsibilities. This process allows landowners to express their views and provide informed consent as a group before the Land Council or a Land Trust makes arrangements that affect the land. This principle is fundamental to the *Aboriginal Land Rights (Northern Territory) Act 1976*. The Northern Land Council also acts as a representative body for native title claimants under the *Native Title Act 1993*.

In 1995 the Northern Land Council created the 'A Caring for Country' unit and it is now one of the Council's largest units. Setting up groups of Aboriginal rangers is an important part of the unit's work. The unit's role in managing both land and sea includes controlling fire, feral weeds and animals, and monitoring endangered special, like turtle and dugong. It also takes an active role in preserving traditional knowledge for future generations. Similar land and sea management units are being established all around the country.

ATSIC was blamed for failures that were outside its responsibilities and obligations.

After the Labor electoral win in November 2007, the new Prime Minister, Kevin Rudd, abolished the National Indigenous Council created by the former federal government and began consultations to establish a new organisation to represent Aboriginal and Torres Strait Islander people at the federal level, with discussion papers being written and considered.

Aboriginal Land Councils are regional organisations made up of people elected from the communities who represent and provide a strong voice for their communities. They help people get back on country, consult with landowners on mining, employment and development, help resolve land disputes and protect Aboriginal culture and sacred sites. Community councils had been established on most islands in the Torres Strait early in 1899. Although they had limited powers, uniquely for the time they were made up of local people. Today the Torres Strait Regional Authority (see p. 84) has twenty elected board members.

The *Mabo* case and the *Native Title Act*

In 1982, Edward Koiki Mabo, along with fellow Mer Islanders (the Reverend Dave Passi, Celuia Salee and James Rice) launched a case in the High Court. In an historic judgment ten years later, the Court held that Meriam people possess rights to their traditional lands and that these rights should be recognised and protected by Australian law. It is often said that the *Mabo* decision overturned the assumption of *terra nullius*: that there were no recognisable Indigenous rights to land before James Cook's arrival in 1788. No longer could it be argued that Australia was a land without law before the arrival of the colonisers. This forced non-Indigenous Australians to confront the injustices of the colonising system.

The Mer Islander action followed the earlier unsuccessful legal action taken in the 1971 Gove land rights *Millirrpum vs Nabalco* case in the Northern Territory Supreme Court. The struggle for our rights to land was fought over decades and the legal challenges have taken their

Bonita Mabo introducing the Mabo Lecture at the AIATSIS NativeTitle Conference (Maabu-garri julu gunganbu-gundi jagunda; The human face of native title), 2005.

toll on the health of our leaders, their non-Indigenous advisers and supporters. There are many cases still to be heard and many elders will not see the day their lands are returned.

After much negotiation and parliamentary debate, the Common-wealth government passed a new law dealing with land rights called the *Native Title Act 1993*. A process was developed to work out whether native title exists in particular areas and how future activity can go ahead when it has an impact on native title. The law also made provisions for

AGREEMENT IS THE WAY TO GO

The South West Land and Sea Council is a native title representative body that works in the interests of the Noongar people of south-west Western Australia. Numbering an estimated 30 000 people, the Noongar are the largest Indigenous group in Australia.

The Council's main role is working with Noongar people to help their native title claims reach a decision by providing legal representation and support, undertaking research and anthropological studies as well as coordinating family claimant meetings. The Council also works to preserve and continue Noongar history, culture and society and, with communities on Caring for Country, manage natural resources.

After lengthy and difficult litigation that eventually resulted in no outcome, the parties are looking to mediation as the next step in the single Noongar claim over Perth. In 2008, CEO Glen Kelly said:

> Let's go to mediation next so we can examine the most sensible way of going forward alongside the six underlying [native title] claims. We need a reasonable, rational approach. We are not going to throw away 60 000 years of lore and culture because someone else thinks it's a good idea. That search for justice will never end because the shadow in our hearts pushes us on.

us to be compensated where our native title is reduced or wiped out. By the end of December 2007, the courts had recognised 74 native title claims, covering a total area of 785 686 square kilometres, with a total of 508 claimant applications still active.

Since the *Mabo* case, decisions made by judges in native title cases and amendments to the law have considerably reduced the potential of the native title law to recognise the rights of all Indigenous people. This has led both Indigenous groups and governments to look to alternative ways of resolving these outstanding issues of land justice. Other methods — rather than court cases — for reaching decisions about land, such as using Indigenous Land Use Agreements (ILUAs), have emerged as a

YOU ARE
LEAVING THE
CANNING
STOCK ROUTE

A sign on the track to
the Calvert Ranges
from the Canning
Stock Route warning
tourists that they are
about to leave the
gazetted road and
enter Martu land in
Western Australia.

strong basis for developing ongoing relationships with government and
industry. By the end of 2007, 310 Indigenous Land Use Agreements
had been registered, including a range of issues like health, education,
governance and land and sea management.

Native title remains a form of 'justice in transition' that needs
careful review to make it a fairer, faster and more workable system for
all. Unfortunately, the process can pitch one set of claimants against
another, creating or intensifying divisions within our communities. With
recognition, however, native title holders enjoy much greater protection
of their rights and interests in their traditional country, which both state
and federal governments must respect. For us, it is not merely a form
of title but a fundamental recognition of our unique identity as the first
peoples of Australia.

Bringing Them Home: Admitting that generations were stolen

The Human Rights and Equal Opportunity Commission Inquiry into the separation of Aboriginal and Torres Strait Islanders from their families was published in the *Bringing Them Home* report (1997). It detailed the laws, policies and practices that allowed our children to be taken from their families, and included many case studies that contest the claim made by many non-Indigenous Australians that the removal of our children was in their own interests.

The exact number of children who were removed may never be known, but the impact of the removals has traumatised our communities and few families have been left unaffected. Almost all of us have had a relative, including close family members, damaged by this policy. Some children were deeply affected by this sudden separation from family and language, many having been told that their families were dead or didn't want them. Some who were institutionalised have grown up into adulthood without the love and nurturing most people take for granted. For many, this has affected their ability to run their own households and bring up their own families. It is very painful to listen to parents and children talk about the effect the removals have had on their lives. Some people in Australia claim the Stolen Generations is a myth, but for us it was a traumatic reality.

Some children benefited from being removed from dysfunctional families but, in general, removal was not in the child's best interests. The institutions and church missions where most 'stolen' children found themselves suppressed their knowledge about their own families, language and culture. In some places discipline was often enforced with heartless and brutal punishments.

Aside from some excellent documentaries on this topic, the mainstream release of the film *Rabbit-Proof Fence* was perhaps the first time that large numbers of Australian cinema-goers learned of the immense pain and hardship caused by the removal policy. The film was based on a book by Doris Pilkington Garimara, who, after being

COMPENSATION FOR STOLEN GENERATIONS

Aged 50, Bruce Trevorrow, whose Ngarrindjeri parents put him into hospital as a child, only to have him fostered out without their knowledge, was awarded compensation, ten years after the *Bringing Them Home* report was tabled.

As a baby, Bruce Trevorrow lived with his parents, Thora Karpany and Joseph Trevorrow, and their family at One Mile Camp, about 150 kilometres from Adelaide. When he was ill, his father sought help from the police and neighbours to get him to hospital.

Despite Trevorrow's recovery, the hospital records declared him a 'neglected child without parents' and he was put in foster care. No one asked his parents for permission. They were not told when or where he was taken and their enquiries about their child were ignored.

Bruce Trevorrow did not meet his natural mother and siblings until he was ten years old, when he was taken to visit them. By then, his behaviour had deteriorated to the point that he was institutionalised. Bruce's life as an adult included unemployment, heavy drinking and unhappy family relationships.

In 1994 Bruce began to ask questions: 'I was just moving from institution to institution. I thought I'd just ask why I ended up in there'.

In August 2007 Justice Gray found that Bruce Trevorrow had been wrongfully removed from his family: 'It was this conduct that ruptured the bond between the plaintiff and his mother and natural family'.

Whereas Bruce Trevorrow had to endure the stress of his case to obtain compensation in South Australia, in 2006 the Tasmanian state government created a $5 million fund to provide payments to eligible members of the Stolen Generations and their children.

Bruce Trevorrow passed away on 20 June 2008, aged 51.

reunited with her mother after decades of separation, learned of her mother and aunts' experience following their removal as children from a desert community. There are many other examples of child removal and institutionalisation. Sister Kate's Home, established in Perth in 1930, received many lighter-skinned children taken from their families by government officials. Much of the pain continues long after we have been reunited with our families, as a result of the length of separation, sometimes as much as forty and fifty years. Link-Up is one of several organisations that now provide support to people searching for their families (see p. 14).

Stolen wages

From the late 1800s and through much of the twentieth century, governments controlled most aspects of our lives and this included our wages, pensions and endowments. Often we received only a portion of what was due to us, with the remainder kept in various trust funds. Much of that money was mismanaged or diverted to other government programs, a fact pointed out to various governments but ignored. Our families were never shown what money was being held and what was owed them. This practice is now called 'stolen wages' and while the Queensland, New South Wales and Western Australian state governments are taking action, for many families it will be a case of 'too little, too late'. In mid-2006, the Commonwealth Parliament set up a Senate inquiry, which provided a report. To date, no action has been taken on the findings.

A Treaty?

Behind all these campaigns the notion of a treaty between Indigenous and non-Indigenous Australia still lingers. There has never been a negotiated settlement to transfer lands and sovereignty from Aboriginal and Torres Strait Islander peoples to the British and now Australian colonial state. Some say this puts a legal question mark over Australia's sovereignty.

The potential legal or moral legitimacy that such an agreement would bring, however, is sometimes seen as secondary to the symbolic or reconciliatory benefits that would result. In particular, for Indigenous people to be formally part of the 'constitutional' make-up of the country would provide a sense of social inclusion that could have a direct impact on the mental wellbeing of individuals, and change the perception of many non-Indigenous Australians about the nature of a shared history and shared future.

It is often thought that it would be too hard to reach agreement on a single national document, and various models of regional approaches have been investigated. For example, constitutional recognition and protection against racial discrimination is often put forward as an alternative to a national treaty, with a system of locally base settlements underpinned by a national framework.

Constitutional recognition of itself may go some way to achieving some of the symbolic purposes of a treaty and protect some basic rights, but it would not go far enough. A treaty, or treaty framework, would be expected to involve a settlement of land and governance issues and could result in greater involvement of some Indigenous communities in the governance of their regions. It would also be likely to involve a more broad based approach to settling land issues, including compensation, than is available through the native title process.

Torres Strait Treaty

The Torres Strait Treaty, an agreement signed in 1978 between Australia and Papua New Guinea, defines the boundaries between the two countries and outlines how the sea area may be used. Besides defining the seabed boundary, it allocates rights over fish between the two countries and protects customary rights, including fishing and free movement across the border, in an area called the 'Protected Zone', which covers about two-thirds of the Torres Strait.

Reconciliation and Celebration

The reconciliation movement began with an effort by Australians to acknowledge the wrongs done to us, to promise that such actions would never be repeated and to adopt measures to repair the pain and loss. Reconciliation requires that Australia acknowledges the manner in which it acquired the land and how it has consistently crushed our attempts to seek common justice. Some of us don't believe we need to be the ones taking the lead in reconciliation; others believe Indigenous and non-Indigenous Australians need to work together. Some non-Indigenous Australians oppose reconciliation or apologies for past practices, believing instead that they are not responsible for the actions of previous generations, or governments.

Bob Hawke, Australian Prime Minister from 1983 to 1991, made a promise, following a second bark petition presented to the Commonwealth Parliament, that his government would work toward a treaty or compact. The government established the Council for Aboriginal Reconciliation (CAR) in 1991 and it operated for ten years to promote reconciliation and advise the government on formal ways by which reconciliation could be achieved.

Groups like Australians for Native Title and Reconciliation (ANTaR) and Reconciliation Australia (RA) work steadily for reconciliation, as did the former Council for Reconciliation headed by Patrick Dodson and Evelyn Scott. Many Australians have participated in the Sea of Hands (a national public art installation where people can sign a hand to reflect their commitment to justice for Australia's Indigenous people), which has travelled around the country. This is an initiative of Australians for Native Title and Reconciliation (ANTaR). In 2000, at the release of the final reports of the CAR many thousands of people walked across Melbourne's Princes Bridge and hundreds of thousands across Sydney's Harbour Bridge, while other states had massive gatherings in a national expression of a desire for reconciliation.

Reconciliation march in Sydney, 28 May 2000,
© Wendy McDougall.

Plans for action

Reconciliation Action Plans permit organisations to build relationships between Indigenous and non-Indigenous Australians. They allow everyone to make a public contribution to the national reconciliation effort. International experience and the growing evidence of what works reveal the essential ingredient: respectful partnerships between Indigenous and non-Indigenous people.

NAIDOC Day

NAIDOC Day is celebrated around the country every July, and it has its origins in the fight for Aboriginal rights that began in the 1920s and 1930s when groups like the Australian Aboriginal Progressive Association and the Australian Aborigines League drew attention to our poor living conditions and our lack of citizenship rights. In 1957, a National Aborigines Day Observance Committee (NADOC) was formed, supported by federal and state governments, the churches and major Indigenous organisations. In 1988 the committee's name was changed to NAIDOC (National Aborigines and Islanders Day Observance Committee) to acknowledge Torres Strait Islander people.

The Apology

The mood of the nation changed on 13 February 2008, when the Prime Minister, Kevin Rudd, and the leader of the Opposition, Brendan Nelson, offered an apology to members of the Stolen Generations, which was supported almost unanimously in the House of Representatives.

Ngarrindjeri singer, Ruby Hunter, performing at NAIDOC Day at the Botanic Gardens in Canberra 1999.

It was an important day for the nation and seemed to release a tide of goodwill and a commitment to right past wrongs and overcome the social disadvantage of Indigenous people, while involving communities in bridging the gap programs. The program of reform is there: jurists, law enforcement agencies, health and welfare agencies and educational experts have made the recommendations.

Some in our country do not believe that the land was taken from us by force, or that dispossession is at the root of the difference between the lives of Indigenous and non-Indigenous Australians today. But most Australians acknowledge that no treaty was entered into. Such an acknowledgment would be a sign of the nation's mature reflection. To bridge the economic and social gap between Indigenous and non-Indigenous Australians is an important moral enterprise. It is also economically sensible because it reduces our need for welfare by drawing more people into jobs. All Australians will be enriched, and all Australians will have been given a fair go.

Prime Minister Kevin Rudd and former Leader of the Opposition, Brendan Nelson, assisting Ngunnawal elder Matilda House don her possum-skin cloak at the end of the Apology ceremony 2008, © Juno Gemes.

Australia

Torres Strait Islands

Festivals and Tours

Most of our Aboriginal and Torres Strait Islander festivals encourage the participation of visitors. Garma in the Northern Territory has been popular for years, while The Dreaming in northern New South Wales is rapidly gaining audiences. Check the Internet and look for festivals in the area you are visiting and prepare to be entertained and informed.

Some of the smaller festivals include the Eel Festival (Victoria), the Laura Dance and Cultural Festival (Queensland) and the Torres Strait Cultural Festival, and there are many more.

Many Australian and overseas visitors are taking advantage of the increasing number of tourist programs operated by our communities. There is no better way to appreciate our cultures than to hear it from us. Visitors can learn about mud-crabbing and trochus jewellery at One Arm Point (western Kimberley, Western Australia) or bush tucker and aquaculture at Lake Condah (Victoria), while contact with rare animals is the daily experience in the Desert Park at Alice Springs. There are rainforest tours at Queensland's Mossman Gorge or guided walks on the Larapinta trail or the Adnyamathana lands of South Australia's Flinders Ranges. There are many groups offering first-class tourism experiences. These are good examples of people staying on their country, within their communities, and teaching and retaining their culture while running a business enterprise.

We also run cultural centres. Koorie Heritage Trust Inc. in Victoria, Tjakupai Aboriginal Cultural Park in Cairns in northern Queensland, Muru Mittigar Aboriginal and Cultural Education Centre in New South Wales and Gab Titui Cultural Centre on Thursday Island in the Torres Strait are some award-winning enterprises. Some of these, like Kooljaman at Cape Leveque in Western Australia, are eco-tourism centres.

Travelling Respectfully

Should you wish to visit our communities, you may find that there are organised tours, in many cases led by Indigenous people. If not, it is advisable to write, phone or fax the Council in any community you wish

The annual Garma Festival is the largest and most vibrant celebration of Yolngu of north-east Arnhem Land and their cultural inheritance.

to visit. There are some communities, especially in remote areas, where you need to seek permission to enter before your visit as it is legally privately held land. This also ensures your safety in remote and difficult terrain, and helps to protect the community from unwelcome intrusions, especially at times of mourning.

Some communities have areas of cultural and spiritual significance that are restricted to the general public, so it is always a good idea to ask whether or not such areas exist in the community you visit. For instance, it is inappropriate to swim in some waterholes and there are other areas that are restricted. Just as many cultures forbid the drinking of alcohol, there are many places in our country where it is not permitted.

As in any society, it important to respect people's privacy and to dress appropriately. Remember, too, that for some Indigenous Australians, English is a second or third language, and the people you speak to may not wish to divulge certain spiritual and cultural matters. Direct and forceful questions can be embarrassing to us. It is courteous to

Martu elders on their country, Great Western Desert, Western Australia.

ask for permission before you take photos or video. If you intend to take or publish photos — even if you just want to post them on your website or networking page — it is a good idea to seek an individual's or community's permission before doing so. Explain how you might want to use the images, and, if commerce is involved, please consider sharing copyright. Obtain the names of the people in the photo or video so you can say who they are, and ask if people want copies of the photos sent to them. Although less common now, there are some communities whose members strenuously avoid seeing images of deceased relatives or hearing them in recordings. They find such reminders of loss very distressing, so it is good to establish whether or not such prohibitions exist in the community you visit.

KEEPING PLACES

The Martu are Western Desert people. They began making contact with frontier whitefellas about eighty years ago and Jigalong was home for most Martu for many decades. More recently, several Martu communities have been established on or near traditional homelands, and today many people continue to live in these desert communities, while others live in towns in the Pilbara region. They retain strong links to their country, their kin and their culture.

A commitment to preserve their culture for their future generations led to *Kanyirninpa Jukurrpa* — a project that uses technology to help preserve and share important information.

The project records oral history from both Martu and whitefellas, and collects archival history. A digital archive of films, photos, slides, tapes and other significant records is now used in every Martu community and school. Genealogies trace modern Martu families back two or three generations prior to their first contact with whitefellas.

The cornerstone is a 'return to country' program where elders take young Martu back to remote parts of their desert lands, to important sites and routes. There they learn, record and look after their country.

Businesses like cultural awareness training, field consulting, communications, natural and cultural resource management, media and publications, are being built on Martu's distinctive, rich intellectual capital.

New opportunities for future generations of Martu and new understanding for mainstream Australians are being created:

Kanyirninpa Jukurrpa martulu palya. Jampa jirlpi miturriku, jijilu malajanulu kanyilku jukurrpa.

(Kanyirninpa Jukurrpa is good for Martu. When the old people are gone, the young people still need to look after jukurrpa.)

Muuki Taylor, Senior Cultural Advisor.

Further reading

We see *The Little Red Yellow Black Book* as a stepping off point for readers to learn more themselves, or with others. The following non-fiction books provide more detail about some of the subjects covered in the book. Because of the limits of space, the list is by no means exhaustive. Australia has an abundance of excellent Indigenous cultural creators and we recommend you explore their work. Our *The Little Red Yellow Black Book* website contains a fuller listing and includes journals, papers, audio-visual materials and websites.

Arthur, W & Morphy, F (eds) 2005, *Macquarie Atlas of Indigenous Australia: Culture and society through space and time*, Macquarie Library, North Ryde, NSW.

Attwood, B 2003, *Rights for Aborigines*, Allen & Unwin, Crows Nest, NSW.

Beresford, Q & Partington, G (eds) 2003, *Reform & Resistance in Aboriginal Education: The Australian experience*, University of Western Australia Press, Nedlands, WA.

Davis, R (ed.) 2003, *Woven Histories, Dancing Lives: Torres Strait Islander identity, culture and history*, Aboriginal Studies Press, Canberra.

Fletcher, E 2004, *Indigenous Family History Research: Family history for beginners and beyond*, Heraldry & Genealogy Society of Canberra, Canberra.

Haebich, A 2000, *Broken Circles: Fragmenting Indigenous families 1800–2000*, Fremantle Arts Centre Press, Fremantle, WA.

Hall, RA 1997, *The Black Diggers: Aborigines and Torres Strait Islanders in the Second World War*, Aboriginal Studies Press, Canberra.

Janke, T & Quiggin, R 2007, *Protocols for producing Indigenous Australian Arts*, 2nd edn, (five booklets) Australia Council for the Arts, Stawberry Hills.

Jupp, J (ed.) 2001, *The Australian People: An encyclopedia of the nation, its people and their origins*, 2nd edn, Cambridge University Press, Oakleigh, Vic.

Kleinert, S & Neale, M (eds) 2000, *The Oxford Companion to Aboriginal Art and Culture*, Oxford University Press, Melbourne, Victoria.

Maynard, J 2007, *Fight for Liberty and Freedom: The origins of Australian Aboriginal activism*, Aboriginal Studies Press, Canberra.

Memmott, P 2007, *Gunyah, Goondie + Wurley: The Aboriginal architecture of Australia*, University of Queensland Press, St Lucia, Qld.

Mulvaney, DJ & White, JP 1987, *Australians to 1788*, Syme & Weldon Associates, Broadway, NSW.

Pascoe, B 2007, *Convincing Ground: Learning to fall in love with your country*, Aboriginal Studies Press, Canberra.

Reynolds, H 2006, *The Other Side of the Frontier: Aboriginal resistance of the European invasion of Australia*, University of New South Wales Press, Sydney.

Taffe, S 2005, *Black and White Together FCAATSI: The Federal Council for the Advancement of Aborigines and Torres Strait Islanders, 1958–1973*, University of Queensland Press, St Lucia, Qld.

Tatz, C & Tatz, P 2000, *Black Gold: The Aboriginal and Islander Sports Hall of Fame*, Aboriginal Studies Press, Canberra.

Thieberger, T & McGregor, W (eds) 1994, *Macquarie Aboriginal Words: A dictionary of words from Australian Aboriginal and Torres Strait Islander languages*, The Macquarie Library Pty Ltd, Sydney.

Acknowledgments

Aboriginal Studies Press would like to acknowledge the assistance and support of the AIATSIS Council, Principal, and the Research, Audio–Visual Archive and Library programs staff. In addition we thank various readers of the manuscript for their insights.

Every attempt has been made to obtain copyright and reproduction permissions for all material sourced. If you believe an image has not been correctly identified or acknowledged, Aboriginal Studies Press, AIATSIS would welcome your feedback (asp@aiatsis.gov.au).

AIATSIS thanks and acknowledges the kind permission to reproduce material (all photographs unless noted otherwise) from the following people: **front cover (top left and ii)** Birrmuyingathi Maali Netta Loogatha, *My Sister Amy's Country* 2007, synthetic polymer paint on linen, 152x101 cm, courtesy the artist, Mornington Island Arts and Crafts, Qld., and Alcaston Gallery, Vic.; **(top centre)** former Essendon footballer Michael Long holds the 1993 AFL Premiership Cup, photo Bruce Magilton, © Newspix, News Ltd, 3rd Party Managed Reproduction & Supply Rights; **(top right)** Christopher Pabai performing at the 2007 Native Title Conference, photo Leigh Harris; **(bottom left)** Bangarra Dance Company, Sydney 2001, Viscopy; © Newspix, News Ltd, 3rd Party Managed Reproduction & Supply Rights; **(bottom centre)** Norbert Japaljarri Spencer being painted for ceremony at Warlukurlangu Artists, Yuendumu, NT; **(bottom right)** photo © Vic Cherikoff (www.cherikoff.net); **back cover (left)** © Vicki Couzens; **(centre)** photo Captain Samuel Sweet, © AIATSIS, ACT; **(right)** Olman Walley performing at the NT conference 2008, photo © Toni Wilkinson; **iv** photo Toni Wilkinson; **4** © Adrian Harris Photography; **6** © Jens-Uwe Korff, www.creativespirits.info; **9** © Charlie Matjuwi, Elcho Island, ochre on paper, 1.5x1m; **11** photo Andy Tyndall, *Herald Sun*, © Newspix, News Ltd, 3rd Party Managed Reproduction & Supply Rights; **12** DB Rose 1996, *Nourishing Terrains: Australian Aboriginal views of landscape and wilderness*, © Australian Heritage Commission, Department of the Environment, Water, Heritage and the Arts, ACT; **13** P D'Arcy, *The Emu in the Sky: Stories about the Aboriginals and the day and night skies*, National Science and Technology Centre, ACT; **15** photo Lyndon Mechielsen, 10368874, © Newspix, News Ltd, 3rd Party Managed Reproduction & Supply Rights; **16** © Haddon Collection, AIATSIS, ACT; **17** M Lawrie, 'Widul and Marte and their brother Umai', *Myth and Legends of Torres Strait*, University of Queensland Press, Qld.; **19** © Luke Taylor; **21** photo Vic Cherikoff (www.cherikoff.net); **23** creator DR Horton, © Aboriginal Studies Press, ACT; **27** © Batchelor Institute of Indigenous Tertiary Education, NT; **29** photo Mark Williams, 06569750 © Newspix, News Ltd, 3rd Party Managed Reproduction & Supply Rights; **30** © Australian Bureau of Statistics, 2006 Census data, creator Geoff Dane; **31** © AIATSIS, ACT, courtesy Papunya Tula Artists, Alice Springs, NT; **33** © Rebecca Lee Hogan-Baker; **34** © South-West Aboriginal Medical Service, courtesy Glenda Hume; **35** © AIATSIS, courtesy Durri Aboriginal Corporation Medical Service; **36** P Memmott 2007, *Gunyah Goondie + Wurley: The Aboriginal architecture of Australia*, University of Queensland Press, Qld © P Memmott; **37** © Gail Mabo; **38** photo Wayne Quilliam, © Yothu Yindi Foundation, Garma Festival, NT; **41** © Graeme K Ward; **42** photo Greg Barrett © William Barton; **45** (top) © Karl Neuenfeldt, thanks to Seaman Dan; (bottom) illus Kathy Fisher © Frank York; **46** © Newspix, News Ltd, 3rd Party Managed Reproduction & Supply Right **48** photo Pauline Clague, Core Films Pty Ltd © Gail Mabo; **49** © Luke Taylor; **51** © Vicki Couzens; **53** courtesy H Chatfield, photo K Styche, AIATSIS © AIATSIS, ACT; **54** photo Kim Batterham © 2000 MusicArtsDance Films Pty Ltd; **56** courtesy Anita Heiss, photo © R Black; **57** National Library of Australia, ACT; **58** courtesy Rachel Bin Salleh; **59** photo Amanda James, courtesy Gavin Jones © National Indigenous Television; **60** © Aboriginal Hostels Ltd, Commonwealth of Australia; **61** Gustav Mützel, Blandowski's *Australien in 142 Photographischen Abbildungen*,

The Little Red Yellow Black Book

Index

First published in 2008 by Aboriginal Studies Press
Reprinted 2009, 2010

© Australian Institute of Aboriginal and Torres Strait Islander Studies 2008

First edition of *The Little Red Yellow Black Book* was published in 1994

Written by Bruce Pascoe with AIATSIS
Published by Aboriginal Studies Press
the publishing arm of the Australian Institute of Aboriginal
and Torres Strait Islander Studies
GPO Box 553, Canberra, ACT 2601
Phone: (61 2) 6246 1183
Fax: (61 2) 6261 4288
Email: asp@aiatsis.gov.au
Web: www.aiatsis.gov.au/aboriginal_studies_press

National Library of Australia
Cataloguing-In-Publication data:

  Title: The little red yellow black book: an introduction to indigenous Australia
  Edition: 2nd ed.
  ISBN: 9780855756154 (pbk.)
  Notes: Includes index.
  Bibliography.
  Subjects: Aboriginal Australians — Social conditions. Torres Strait Islanders--Social conditions. Aboriginal Australian — Social life and customs. Torres Strait Islanders — Social life and customs. Other Authors/Contributors: Australian Institute of Aboriginal and Torres Strait Islander Studies.
Dewey Number: 305.89915

Printed in China by Phoenix Offset Pty Ltd